studysync®

Reading & Writing Companion

Epic Heroes

studysync

studysync.com

Send all inquiries to:
BookheadEd Learning, LLC
610 Daniel Young Drive
Sonoma, CA 95476

5 6 7 8 9 LMN 22

G12U1

STUDENT GUIDE

GETTING STARTED

Welcome to the StudySync Reading and Writing Companion! In this booklet, you will find a collection of readings based on the theme of the unit you are studying. As you work through the readings, you will be asked to answer questions and perform a variety of tasks designed to help you closely analyze and understand each text selection. Read on for an explanation of each section of this booklet.

CORE ELA TEXTS

In each Core ELA Unit you will read texts and text excerpts that share a common theme, despite their different genres, time periods, and authors. Each reading encourages a closer look with questions and a short writing assignment.

INTRODUCTION

An Introduction to each text provides historical context for your reading as well as information about the author. You will also learn about the genre of the excerpt and the year in which it was written.

FIRST READ

During your first reading of each excerpt, you should just try to get a general idea of the content and message of the reading. Don't worry if there are parts you don't understand or words that are unfamiliar to you. You'll have an opportunity later to dive deeper into the text.

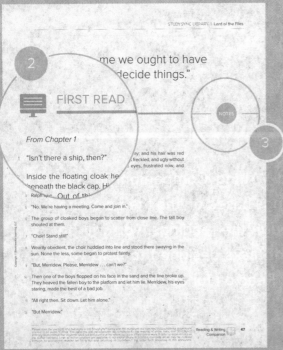

NOTES

Many times, while working through the activities after each text, you will be asked to **annotate** or **make annotations** about what you are reading. This means that you should highlight or underline words in the text and use the "Notes" column to make comments or jot down any questions you may have. You may also want to note any unfamiliar vocabulary words here.

THINK QUESTIONS

These questions will ask you to start thinking critically about the text, asking specific questions about its purpose, and making connections to your prior knowledge and reading experiences. To answer these questions, you should go back to the text and draw upon specific evidence that you find there to support your responses. You will also begin to explore some of the more challenging vocabulary words used in the excerpt.

CLOSE READ & FOCUS QUESTIONS

After you have completed the First Read, you will then be asked to go back and read the excerpt more closely and critically. Before you begin your Close Read, you should read through the Focus Questions to get an idea of the concepts you will want to focus on during your second reading. You should work through the Focus Questions by making annotations, highlighting important concepts, and writing notes or questions in the "Notes" column. Depending on instructions from your teacher, you may need to respond online or use a separate piece of paper to start expanding on your thoughts and ideas.

WRITING PROMPT

Your study of each excerpt or selection will end with a writing assignment. To complete this assignment, you should use your notes, annotations, and answers to both the Think and Focus Questions. Be sure to read the prompt carefully and address each part of it in your writing assignment.

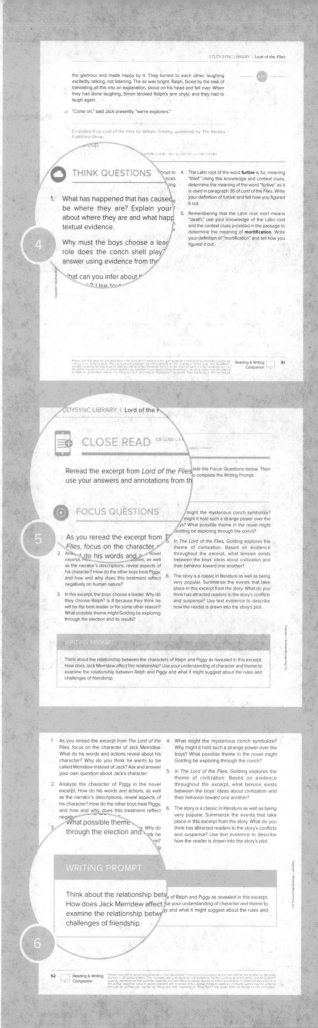

ENGLISH LANGUAGE DEVELOPMENT TEXTS

The English Language Development texts and activities take a closer look at the language choices that authors make to communicate their ideas. Individual and group activities will help develop your understanding of each text.

1 REREAD

After you have completed the First Read, you will have two additional opportunities to revisit portions of the excerpt more closely. The directions for each reread will specify which paragraphs or sections you should focus on.

2 USING LANGUAGE

These questions will ask you to analyze the author's use of language and conventions in the text. You may be asked to write in sentence frames, fill in a chart, or you may simply choose between multiple-choice options. To answer these questions, you should read the exercise carefully and go back in the text as necessary to accurately complete the activity.

3 MEANINGFUL INTERACTIONS & SELF-ASSESSMENT RUBRIC

After each reading, you will participate in a group activity or discussion with your peers. You may be provided speaking frames to guide your discussions or writing frames to support your group work. To complete these activities, you should revisit the excerpt for textual evidence and support. When you finish, use the Self-Assessment Rubric to evaluate how well you participated and collaborated.

EXTENDED WRITING PROJECT

The Extended Writing Project is your opportunity to explore the theme of each unit in a longer written work. You will draw information from your readings, research, and own life experiences to complete the assignment.

1 WRITING PROJECT

After you have read all of the unit text selections, you will move on to a writing project. Each project will guide you through the process of writing an argumentative, narrative, informative, or literary analysis essay. Student models and graphic organizers will provide guidance and help you organize your thoughts as you plan and write your essay. Throughout the project, you will also study and work on specific writing skills to help you develop different portions of your writing.

2 WRITING PROCESS STEPS

There are five steps in the writing process: **Prewrite**, **Plan**, **Draft**, **Revise**, and **Edit, Proofread, and Publish**. During each step, you will form and shape your writing project so that you can effectively express your ideas. Lessons focus on one step at a time, and you will have the chance to receive feedback from your peers and teacher.

3 WRITING SKILLS

Each Writing Skill lesson focuses on a specific strategy or technique that you will use during your writing project. The lessons begin by analyzing a student model or mentor text, and give you a chance to learn and practice the skill on its own. Then, you will have the opportunity to apply each new skill to improve the writing in your own project.

UNIT 1   Where does history end and legend begin?

Epic Heroes

TEXTS

ENGLISH LANGUAGE DEVELOPMENT TEXTS

EXTENDED WRITING PROJECT

BEOWULF
(LINES 1325–1477)

POETRY
Anglo-Saxon Tradition
8th to 11th Century

INTRODUCTION

studysync tv

The author, date of composition, and inspiration of "Beowulf" are unknown, but its place as an archetypal Anglo-Saxon text and oldest surviving epic poem in English is indisputable. For 12 years the people of Denmark under the leadership of King Hrothgar are terrorized by a brutal monster named Grendel. When Beowulf, hero of the Geats, learns of this, he decides to repay a favor to Hrothgar by slaying the beast. Little does he know that he will also have to contend with the monster's mother.

"Ride we anon, and mark the trail of the mother of Grendel."

FIRST READ

XX

1325. HROTHGAR spake, helmet-of-Scyldings:—
1326. "Ask not of pleasure! Pain is renewed
1327. to Danish folk. Dead is Aeschere,
1328. of Yrmenlaf the elder brother,
1329. my sage adviser and stay in council,
1330. shoulder-comrade in stress of fight
1331. when warriors clashed and we warded our heads,
1332. hewed the helm-boars; hero famed
1333. should be every earl as Aeschere was!
1334. But here in Heorot a hand hath slain him
1335. of wandering death-sprite. I wot not whither,
1336. proud of the prey, her path she took,
1337. fain of her fill. The feud she **avenged**
1338. that yesternight, unyieldingly,
1339. Grendel in grimmest grasp thou killedst,—
1340. seeing how long these liegemen mine
1341. he ruined and **ravaged.** Reft of life,
1342. in arms he fell. Now another comes,
1343. keen and cruel, her kin to avenge,
1344. faring far in feud of blood:
1345. so that many a thane shall think, who e'er
1346. sorrows in soul for that sharer of rings,
1347. this is hardest of heart-bales. The hand lies low
1348. that once was willing each wish to please.
1349. Land-dwellers here and liegemen mine,
1350. who house by those parts, I have heard relate
1351. that such a pair they have sometimes seen,
1352. march-stalkers mighty the moorland haunting,
1353. wandering spirits: one of them seemed,

NOTES

1354. so far as my folk could fairly judge,
1355. of womankind; and one, accursed,
1356. in man's guise trod the misery-track
1357. of exile, though huger than human bulk.
1358. Grendel in days long gone they named him,
1359. folk of the land; his father they knew not,
1360. nor any brood that was born to him
1361. of **treacherous** spirits. Untrod is their home;
1362. by wolf-cliffs haunt they and windy headlands,
1363. fenways fearful, where flows the stream
1364. from mountains gliding to gloom of the rocks,
1365. underground flood. Not far is it hence
1366. in measure of miles that the mere expands,
1367. and o'er it the frost-bound forest hanging,
1368. sturdily rooted, shadows the wave.
1369. By night is a wonder weird to see,
1370. fire on the waters. So wise lived none
1371. of the sons of men, to search those depths!
1372. Nay, though the heath-rover, harried by dogs,
1373. the horn-proud hart, this holt should seek,
1374. long distance driven, his dear life first
1375. on the brink he yields ere he brave the plunge
1376. to hide his head: 'tis no happy place!
1377. Thence the welter of waters washes up
1378. wan to welkin when winds bestir
1379. evil storms, and air grows dusk,
1380. and the heavens weep. Now is help once more
1381. with thee alone! The land thou knowst not,
1382. place of fear, where thou findest out
1383. that sin-flecked being. Seek if thou dare!
1384. I will reward thee, for waging this fight,
1385. with ancient treasure, as erst I did,
1386. with winding gold, if thou winnest back."

XXI

1387. BEOWULF spake, bairn of Ecgtheow:
1388. "Sorrow not, sage! It beseems us better
1389. friends to avenge than **fruitlessly** mourn them.
1390. Each of us all must his end abide
1391. in the ways of the world; so win who may
1392. glory ere death! When his days are told,
1393. that is the warrior's worthiest doom.
1394. Rise, O realm-warder! Ride we anon,
1395. and mark the trail of the mother of Grendel.

Reading & Writing
Companion

NOTES

1396. No harbor shall hide her—heed my promise!—
1397. enfolding of field or forested mountain
1398. or floor of the flood, let her flee where she will!
1399. But thou this day endure in patience,
1400. as I ween thou wilt, thy woes each one."
1401. Leaped up the graybeard: God he thanked,
1402. mighty Lord, for the man's brave words.
1403. For Hrothgar soon a horse was saddled
1404. wave-maned steed. The sovran wise
1405. stately rode on; his shield-armed men
1406. followed in force. The footprints led
1407. along the woodland, widely seen,
1408. a path o'er the plain, where she passed, and trod
1409. the murky moor; of men-at-arms
1410. she bore the bravest and best one, dead,
1411. him who with Hrothgar the homestead ruled.
1412. On then went the atheling-born
1413. o'er stone-cliffs steep and strait defiles,
1414. narrow passes and unknown ways,
1415. headlands sheer, and the haunts of the Nicors.
1416. Foremost he fared, a few at his side
1417. of the wiser men, the ways to scan,
1418. till he found in a flash the forested hill
1419. hanging over the hoary rock,
1420. a woful wood: the waves below
1421. were dyed in blood. The Danish men
1422. had sorrow of soul, and for Scyldings all,
1423. for many a hero, 'twas hard to bear,
1424. ill for earls, when Aeschere's head
1425. they found by the flood on the foreland there.
1426. Waves were welling, the warriors saw,
1427. hot with blood; but the horn sang oft
1428. battle-song bold. The band sat down,
1429. and watched on the water worm-like things,
1430. sea-dragons strange that sounded the deep,
1431. and nicors that lay on the ledge of the ness—
1432. such as oft essay at hour of morn
1433. on the road-of-sails their ruthless quest,—
1434. and sea-snakes and monsters. These started away,
1435. swollen and savage that song to hear,
1436. that war-horn's blast. The warden of Geats,
1437. with bolt from bow, then balked of life,
1438. of wave-work, one monster, amid its heart
1439. went the keen war-shaft; in water it seemed
1440. less doughty in swimming whom death had seized.

NOTES

1441. Swift on the billows, with boar-spears well
1442. hooked and barbed, it was hard beset,
1443. done to death and dragged on the headland,
1444. wave-roamer wondrous. Warriors viewed
1445. the grisly guest.
1446. Then girt him Beowulf
1447. in martial mail, nor mourned for his life.
1448. His breastplate broad and bright of hues,
1449. woven by hand, should the waters try;
1450. well could it ward the warrior's body
1451. that battle should break on his breast in vain
1452. nor harm his heart by the hand of a foe.
1453. And the helmet white that his head protected
1454. was destined to dare the deeps of the flood,
1455. through wave-whirl win: 'twas wound with chains,
1456. decked with gold, as in days of yore
1457. the weapon-smith worked it wondrously,
1458. with swine-forms set it, that swords nowise,
1459. **brandished** in battle, could bite that helm.
1460. Nor was that the meanest of mighty helps
1461. which Hrothgar's orator offered at need:
1462. "Hrunting" they named the hilted sword,
1463. of old-time heirlooms easily first;
1464. iron was its edge, all etched with poison,
1465. with battle-blood hardened, nor blenched it at fight
1466. in hero's hand who held it ever,
1467. on paths of peril prepared to go
1468. to folkstead of foes. Not first time this
1469. it was destined to do a daring task.
1470. For he bore not in mind, the bairn of Ecglaf
1471. sturdy and strong, that speech he had made,
1472. drunk with wine, now this weapon he lent
1473. to a stouter swordsman. Himself, though, durst not
1474. under welter of waters wager his life
1475. as loyal liegeman. So lost he his glory,
1476. honor of earls. With the other not so,
1477. who girded him now for the grim encounter.

THINK QUESTIONS CA-CCSS: CA.RL.11-12.1, CA.L.11-12.4a, CA.L.11-12.4d

1. Note in chronological order the two acts of revenge that Hrothgar describes in section XX. For each act, explain who killed who and why they did it, and supply the textual evidence from Hrothgar's speech that confirms the event.

2. Supply three examples of imagery from section XX that support the inference that the region where Grendel and his mother live is a sinister place.

3. Explain what Beowulf is preparing to do at the beginning of section XXI, and describe what values underlie his decision. Cite textual evidence in your response.

4. Review lines 1387 to 1398. Use context to determine the meaning of the word **avenge**. Explain how context helped you determine the meaning of the word.

5. Use the context clue provided in section XX of the passage to guess at the meaning of **ravaged**. Verify your preliminary determination of the meaning by checking in a dictionary. Then write down the definition of *ravaged,* identify the part of speech used in the text, and describe the context clue in the text.

CLOSE READ

CA-CCSS: CA.RL.11-12.1, CA.RL.11-12.3, CA.W.11-12.4, CA.W.11-12.5, CA.W.11-12.6, CA.W.11-12.9a, CA.W.11-12.10, CA.L.11-12.4, CA.L.11-12.5a

Reread the lines from the poem *Beowulf*. As you reread, complete the Focus Questions below. Then use your answers and annotations from the questions to help you complete the Writing Prompt.

 FOCUS QUESTIONS

1. In lines 1372–1376, describe how the setting affects plot development in the scenes in which Beowulf, Hrothgar, and the search party hunt for the home of Grendel and his mother. Highlight and annotate textual evidence to explain your ideas.

2. How would you describe Beowulf's code of behavior? How does the character of Beowulf affect the plot? Highlight and annotate textual evidence in lines 1390–1393 to explain your ideas.

3. Highlight a word that is unfamiliar to you and that is interfering with your comprehension of the text. Then use one or more strategies to determine the meaning of the word. Write a definition of the word, describe how you determined the word's meaning, and explain how knowing the definition helps you better understand the text. Use the annotation tool to write your response to these questions.

4. Find an example of hyperbole associated with Beowulf's sword. Highlight evidence in the text and use the annotation tool to explain how the passages you've chosen propel the plot forward.

5. Recall the unit's Essential Question: Where does history end and legend begin? *Beowulf* features both historical and mythical elements. What inferences can you make about medieval Scandinavia based on the poem? In the poem, where does history end and legend begin? Highlight textual evidence and make annotations to explain your ideas.

WRITING PROMPT

How does a combination of character, plot, and setting in this excerpt from *Beowulf* help you understand the Anglo-Saxon worldview and culture? Use your understanding of story elements to analyze the passage and describe what the literary elements suggest about the underlying beliefs, values, and concerns of the culture *Beowulf* originated from.

Reading & Writing Companion

GRENDEL

FICTION
John Gardner
1971

INTRODUCTION

Grendel is a modern retelling of *Beowulf* from the monster's point of view. In this excerpt, King Hrothgar has built a giant meadhall (a large building with a single room for feasting and entertainment) and is hosting a celebration. As the outcast Grendel observes the festivities, bemoaning his brutish nature, he notes the irony of the humans' heroic perception of themselves—a perception created through the power of art and imagination, as represented by the character of the Shaper, the poet bard of Hrothgar's court.

"I backed away, crablike, further into darkness..."

FIRST READ

Excerpt from Chapter 4

1   Inspired by winds (or whatever you please), the old man sang of a glorious meadhall whose light would shine to the ends of the ragged world. The thought took seed in Hrothgar's mind. It grew. He called all his people together and told them his daring scheme. He would build a magnificent meadhall high on a hill, with a view of the western sea, a victory-seat near the giants' work, old ruined fortress from the world's first war, to stand forever as a sign of the glory and justice of Hrothgar's Danes. There he would sit and give treasures out, all wealth but the lives of men and the people's land. And so his sons would do after him, and his sons' sons, to the final generation.

2   I listened, huddled in the darkness, tormented, mistrustful. I knew them, had watched them; yet the things he said seemed true. He sent to far kingdoms for woodsmen, carpenters, metalsmiths, goldsmiths—also carters, victualers, clothiers to attend to the workmen—and for weeks their uproar filled the days and nights. I watched from the vines and boulders of the giants' ruin, two miles off. Then word went out to the races of men that Hrothgar's hall was finished. He gave it its name. From neighboring realms and from across the sea came men to the great celebration. The harper sang.

3   I listened, felt myself swept up. I knew very well that all he said was ridiculous, not light for their darkness but flattery, illusion, a **vortex** pulling them from sunlight to heat, a kind of midsummer **burgeoning,** waltz to the sickle. Yet I was swept up. "Ridiculous!" I hissed in the black of the forest. I snatched up a snake from beside my foot and whispered to it, "I knew him when!" But I couldn't bring out a wicked cackle, as I'd meant to do. My heart was light with Hrothgar's goodness, and leaden with grief at my own bloodthirsty ways. I backed away, crablike, further into darkness—like a crab retreating in pain when you strike two stones at the mouth of his underwater den. I backed away till the honeysweet lure of the harp no longer mocked me. Yet even

now my mind was tormented by images. Thanes filled the hall and a great silent crowd of them spilled out over the surrounding hill, smiling, peaceable, hearing the harper as if not a man in all that lot had ever twisted a knife in his neighbor's chest.

4 "Well then he's changed them," I said, and stumbled and fell on the root of a tree. "Why not?

5 Why not? the forest whispered back—yet not the forest, something deeper, an impression from another mind, some live thing old and terrible.

6 I listened, tensed.

7 Not a sound.

8 "He reshapes the world," I whispered, **belligerent.** "So his name implies. He stares strange-eyed at the mindless world and turns dry sticks to gold."

9 A little poetic, I would readily admit. His manner of speaking was infecting me, making me **pompous.** "Nevertheless," I whispered crossly—but I couldn't go on, too conscious all at once of my whispering, my eternal posturing, always transforming the world with words—changing nothing. I still had the snake in my fist. I set it down. It fled.

10 "He takes what he finds," I said stubbornly, trying again, "And by changing men's minds he makes the best of it. Why not?" But it sounded **petulant;** and it wasn't true, I knew. He sang for pay, for the praise of women—one in particular—and for the honor of a famous king's hand on his arm. If the ideas of art were beautiful, that was art's fault, not the Shaper's. A blind selector, almost mindless: a bird. Did they murder each other more gently because in the woods sweet songbirds sang?

...

11 Men and women stood talking in the light of the meadhall door and on the narrow streets below; on the lower hillside boys and girls played near the sheep pens, shyly holding hands. A few lay touching each other in the forest eaves. I thought how they'd shriek if I suddenly showed my face, and it made me smile, but I held myself back. They talked nothing, stupidities, their soft voices groping like hands. I felt myself tightening, cross, growing restless for no clear reason, and I made myself move more slowly. Then, circling the clearing, I stepped on something fleshy, and jerked away. It was a man. They'd cut his throat. His clothes had been stolen. I stared up at the hall, baffled, beginning to shake. They went on talking softly, touching hands, their hair full of light. I lifted up the body and slung it across my shoulder.

12   Then the harp began to play. The crowd grew still.

13   The harp sighed, the old man sang, as sweet-voiced as a child.

14   He told how the earth was first built, long ago: said that the greatest gods made the world, every wonder-bright plain and the turning seas, and set out as signs of his victory the sun and moon, great lamps for light to land-dwellers, kingdom torches, and **adorned** the fields with all colors and shapes, made limbs and leaves and gave life to every creature that moves on land.

15   The harp turned solemn. He told of an ancient feud between two brothers which split all the world between darkness and light. And I, Grendel, was the dark side, he said in effect. The terrible race God cursed.

16   I believed him. Such was the power of the Shaper's harp! Stood wriggling my face, letting tears down my nose, grinding my fists into my streaming eyes, even though to do it I had to squeeze with my elbow the corpse of the proof that both of us were cursed, or neither, that the brothers had never lived, nor the god who judged them. "Waaa!" I bawled.

17   Oh what a conversion!

18   I staggered out into the open and up toward the hall with my burden, groaning out, "Mercy! Peace!" The harper broke off, the people screamed. (They have their own versions, but this is the truth.) Drunken men rushed me with battle-axes. I sank to my knees, crying. "Friend! Friend!" They hacked at me, yipping like dogs. I held up the body for protection. Their spears came through it and one of them nicked me, a tiny scratch high on my left breast, but I knew by the sting it had venom on it and I understood, as shocked as I'd been the first time, that they could kill me—eventually would if I gave them a chance. I struck at them, holding the body as a shield, and two fell bleeding from my nails at the first little swipe. The others backed off. I crushed the body in my hug, then hurled it in their faces, turned, and fled. They didn't follow.

Excerpted from Grendel *by John Gardner, published by Vintage Books.*

THINK QUESTIONS
CA-CCSS: CA.RL.11-12.1, CA.L.11-12.4a, CA.L.11-12.4b

1. Where are the Danes during most of this excerpt? Where is Grendel? What do the two different settings suggest about their different places in society? Cite textual evidence to support your answer.

2. Find two words or phrases in the text that best describe Grendel, and explain why you chose them. Use evidence from the text to support your explanations.

3. How does Grendel react to the harp player? Support your answer using evidence from the text.

4. The prefix "vor-" means to "eat greedily." For example, the word "voracious" means "ravenous" and "insatiable," both words having to do with the idea of greed. Based on this information, what would you predict is the meaning of the word **vortex**, as used in *Grendel*? Look for any context clues that support your response. Then explain how the prefix and the context helped you decide what the word means.

5. Identify a context clue in the text that suggests the meaning of the word **adorned** as it is used in *Grendel*. Using that context clue, write your definition of *adorned* here.

CLOSE READ
CA-CCSS: CA.RL.11-12.1, CA.RL.11-12.2, CA.RL.11-12.7, CA.W.11-12.4, CA.W.11-12.5, CA.W.11-12.6, CA.W.11-12.9a, CA.W.11-12.10, CA.L.11-12.4a, CA.L.11-12.4d, CA.L.11-12.5a

Reread the excerpt from *Grendel*. As you reread, complete the Focus Questions below. Then use your answers and annotations from the questions to help you complete the Writing Prompt.

FOCUS QUESTIONS

1. How does the excerpt from *Grendel* introduce the theme of human sinfulness? How does Grendel's discovery of the corpse further develop this theme? Highlight textual evidence, and use the annotation tool to explain how the text you've highlighted helps you answer these questions.

2. Themes of good versus evil and the power of song are introduced in the excerpt from *Grendel*. How do these two themes interact and build on one another to produce a complex account? Highlight textual evidence, and use the annotation tool to explain how the text you've highlighted helps you answer this question.

3. How is Hrothgar described in the excerpts from *Beowulf* and *Grendel*? How is the relationship between Hrothgar and Grendel different in the two works? What is the connection between the relationship depicted in each work and the theme of good versus evil? Highlight textual evidence in both selections, and use the annotation tool to explain how the text you've highlighted helps you answer these questions.

4. Highlight a word in *Grendel* whose precise meaning you do not know. Then use one or more strategies to determine the word's meaning. Write a definition of the word, describe how you determined the word's meaning, and explain how knowing the definition helps you better understand the text. Use the annotation tool to write your response to these questions.

5. Recall that **hyperbole** is a figure of speech that uses exaggeration to express a strong emotion, make a point, or evoke humor. Identify and highlight an example of hyperbole in the first paragraph from *Grendel*. Use the annotation tool to explain the figure of speech and how it develops theme.

6. The Essential Question of this unit asks, "Where does history end and legend begin?" Written in 1971, *Grendel* depicts a creature that is both similar to and different from the monster of the same name in the early medieval text *Beowulf*. Where does the historical conception of Grendel end and a new legend begin in the updated version of the story? Highlight textual evidence in both selections, and use the annotation tool to support your response.

WRITING PROMPT

Many works of literature explore the position of "outsiders" in society, and the character Grendel is one of the most well-known literary outsiders. What comment does the novel *Grendel* make about being an outsider? How does Grendel's outsider status relate to the themes of the pain of isolation, good versus evil, and the power of art to misrepresent reality? Refer to textual evidence from both the novel and the poem to analyze what Gardner expresses about outsiders through his portrayal of the monster Grendel.

THE ECCLESIASTICAL HISTORY OF THE ENGLISH PEOPLE

NON-FICTION
Venerable Bede
731

INTRODUCTION

The Venerable Bede was a monk who lived in England during the Anglo-Saxon period. He was a skilled linguist whose translation of the Greek and Latin works of early Church fathers helped pave the way for Christianity in England. He was also a prolific author and earned the title "The Father of English History" with his masterpiece, *The Ecclesiastical History of the English People*, which documents the influence of the church on the development of English civilization. In this excerpt, King Edwin converts to Christianity after being encouraged by the religious counselor Paulinus and conferring with his trusted chiefs.

"...receive the faith and keep the commandments of Him who rescued you from your earthly foes..."

FIRST READ

The Anglo-Saxons Embrace Christianity

1   King Edwin hesitated to accept the word of God which Paulinus preached but, as we have said, used to sit alone for hours at a time, earnestly debating within himself what he ought to do and what religion he should follow. One day Paulinus came to him and, placing his right hand on the king's head, asked him if he recognized this sign.

2   The king began to tremble and would have thrown himself at the bishop's feet but Paulinus raised him up and said in a voice that seemed familiar, "First you have escaped with God's help from the hands of the foes you feared; secondly you have acquired by His gift the kingdom you desired; do not delay in fulfilling it but receive the faith and keep the commandments of Him who rescued you from your earthly foes and raised you to the honor of an earthly kingdom. If from henceforth you are willing to follow His will which is made known to you through me, He will also rescue you from the everlasting torments of the wicked and make you a partaker with Him of His eternal kingdom of heaven."

3   When the king had heard his words, he answered that he was both willing and bound to accept the faith which Paulinus taught. He said, however, that he would confer about this with his loyal chief men and his counsellors so that, if they agreed with him, they might all be **consecrated** together in the waters of life. Paulinus agreed, and the king did as he had said. A meeting of his council was held, and each one was asked in turn what he thought of this **doctrine** hitherto unknown to them and this new worship of God which was being proclaimed.

4   Coifi, the chief of the priests, answered at once, "Notice carefully, King, this doctrine which is now being **expounded** to us. I frankly admit that, for my part, I have found that the religion which we have hitherto held has no virtue nor

Reading & Writing Companion

NOTES

profit in it. None of your followers has devoted himself more earnestly than I have to the worship of our gods, but nevertheless there are many who receive greater benefits and greater honor from you than I do and are more successful in all their undertakings. If the gods had any power, they would have helped me more readily, seeing that I have always served them with greater zeal. So it follows that if, on examination, these new doctrines which have now been explained to us are found to be better and more effectual, let us accept them at once without any delay."

5   Another of the king's chief men agreed with this advice and with these wise words and then added, "This is how the present life of man on earth, King, appears to me in comparison with that time which is unknown to us. You are sitting feasting with your eldermen and thanes in winter time; the fire is burning on the hearth in the middle of the hall and all inside is warm, while outside the wintry storms of rain and snow are raging; and a sparrow flies swiftly through the hall. It enters in at one door and quickly flies out through the other. For the few moments it is inside, the storm and wintry tempest cannot touch it, but after the briefest moment of calm, it flits from your sight, out of the wintry storm and into it again. So this life of man appears but for a moment; what follows or indeed what went before, we know not at all. If this new doctrine brings us more certain information, it seems right that we should accept it." Other elders and counsellors of the king continued in the same manner, being divinely prompted to do so.

6   Coifi added that he would like to listen still more carefully to what Paulinus himself had to say about God. The king ordered Paulinus to speak, and when he had said his say, Coifi exclaimed, "For a long time now I have realized that our religion is worthless; for the more diligently I sought the truth in our cult, the less I found it. Now I confess openly that the truth shines out clearly in this teaching which can bestow on us the gift of life, salvation, and eternal happiness. Therefore, I advise your Majesty that we should promptly abandon and commit to the flames the temples and the altars which we have held sacred without reaping any benefit." Why need I say more? The king publicly accepted the gospel which Paulinus preached, renounced idolatry, and confessed his faith in Christ. When he asked the high priest of their religion which of them should be the first to **profane** the altars and the shrines of the idols, together with their precincts, Coifi answered, "I will; for through the wisdom the true God has given me no one can more suitably destroy those things which I once foolishly worshipped, and so set an example to all." And at once, casting aside his vain superstitions, he asked the king to provide him with arms and a stallion; and mounting it, he set out to destroy the idols. Now a high priest of their religion was not allowed to carry arms or to ride except on a mare. So, girded with a sword, he took a spear in his hand, and mounting the king's stallion, he set off to where the idols were. The common people who saw him thought he was mad. But as soon as he approached the shrine,

without any hesitation he profaned it by casting the spear which he held into it; and greatly rejoicing in the knowledge of the worship of the true God, he ordered his companions to destroy and set fire to the shrine and all the enclosures. The place where the idols once stood is still shown, not far from York, to the east, over the river Derwent. Today it is called Goodmanham, the place where the high priest, through the inspiration of the true God, profaned and destroyed the altars which he himself had consecrated.

THINK QUESTIONS CA-CCSS: CA.RI.11-12.1, CA.L.11-12.4a

1. Describe the order of events in the selection. What does King Edwin decide to do, and why does he call his council? What is the result of these events? Support your answer with evidence from the text.

2. Who is Coifi? What reasons does he give for converting to Christianity? Why is his support of the King's conversion especially important? Cite textual evidence to support your responses.

3. What is the author's point of view on the conversion of King Edwin and his council? What words and phrases does he use that provide clues to his point of view? What does the author's point of view reveal about the role of religion in Anglo-Saxon England? Cite specific examples in your answer.

4. Use context to determine the meaning of the word **profane** as it is used in *The Ecclesiastical History of the English People*. Note the term is used more than once. Write your definition of *profane* and explain how context helped you determine the definition.

5. Use context to determine the meaning of the word **doctrine** as it is used in *The Ecclesiastical History of the English People*. Note the term is used more than once. Write your definition of *doctrine* here and explain how context helped you determine the definition.

CLOSE READ
CA-CCSS: CA.RI.11-12.1, CA.RI.11-12.3, CA.RI.11-12.4, CA.W.11-12.4, CA.W.11-12.5, CA.W.11-12.6, CA.W.11-12.9b, CA.W.11-12.10, CA.L.11-12.4b, CA.L.11-12.5a

Reread the excerpt from *The Ecclesiastical History of the English People*. As you reread, complete the Focus Questions below. Then use your answers and annotations from the questions to help you complete the Writing Prompt.

FOCUS QUESTIONS

1. In paragraph 1, what conflict is Edwin facing? How do you know that he is struggling internally with this conflict? Highlight evidence in the text and use the annotation tool to explain how the passages you've chosen help you respond to the questions.

2. In paragraph 3, how does Edwin respond when Paulinus tries to convince him to convert to Christianity? What does this reaction reveal about him as a ruler? Highlight evidence in the text and use the annotation tool to explain how the passages you've chosen help you respond to the questions.

3. In paragraph 5, one of King Edwin's councilmen uses an analogy. What two things are being compared? What is the purpose of this analogy? Highlight evidence in the text and use the annotation tool to explain how the passages you've chosen help you respond to the questions.

4. In the last paragraph, how and why does Coifi's role change? Highlight evidence in the text and use the annotation tool to explain how the passages you've chosen help you respond to the question.

5. Find and highlight the word *idol* in the text. Then find and highlight the other form of *idol* used in the text. What is the part of speech and meaning of *idol*? How does the suffix added to the second form affect the part of speech and meaning? Use the annotation tool to respond to these questions.

6. Recall the Essential Question for this unit: Where does history end and legend begin? *The Ecclesiastical History of the English People* is a nonfiction text, but the line between historical fact and legend was not as important when Bede was writing as it is today. In what ways does Bede's account seem more legendary than fact based? Consider the details Bede includes and what you know about how political and religious conflicts were solved during the time period. Highlight evidence in the text to support your response.

WRITING PROMPT

How do individuals, events, and ideas interact and develop over the course of the excerpt from *The Ecclesiastical History of the English People*? What do these interactions and developments reveal about the Anglo-Saxons and the history of Christianity? Use your understanding of informational text elements to support your response. Cite textual evidence to support your analysis.

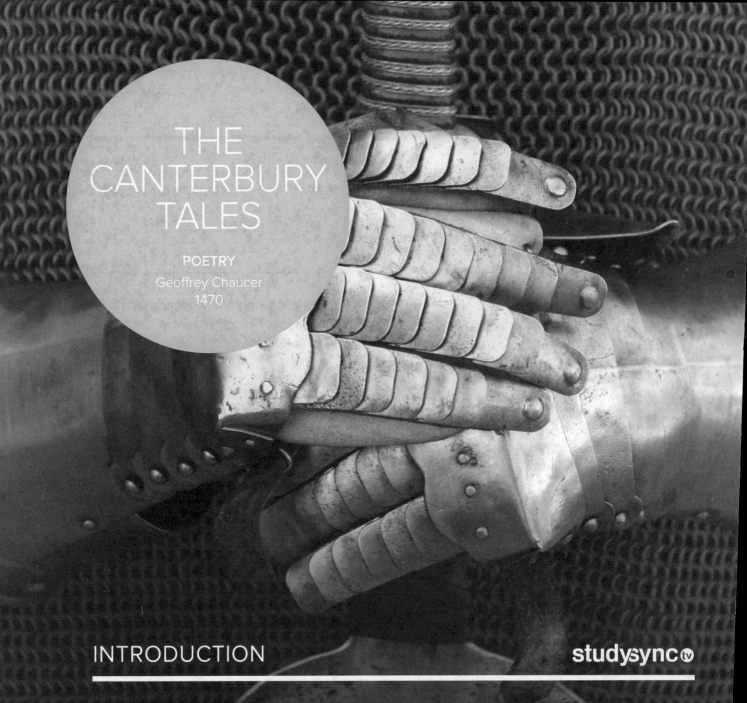

THE CANTERBURY TALES

POETRY
Geoffrey Chaucer
1470

INTRODUCTION

In Geoffrey Chaucer's 14th Century poem, the narrator joins 29 travelers on a pilgrimage from London to Canterbury Cathedral to pay homage to St. Thomas Becket. Telling stories along their journey, with the best tale winning a prize of a free dinner, the pilgrims compete with colorful characters and magical plots. The Wife of Bath, a prosperous widow married five times, tells the tale of a young knight who commits a heinous crime and is sentenced to death. If, by the end of a year and a day, the knight can name the one thing that women truly want, the queen will commute his sentence. On his quest, the knight meets an old woman who holds the answer to the riddle. Accepting her conditions to ensure his freedom, he is beholden to grant her one special request.

"I'll grant you life if you can tell to me What thing it is that women most desire."

 FIRST READ

NOTES

FROM THE PROLOGUE

1 Here begins the Book of the Tales of Canterbury

2 When April with his showers sweet with fruit
3 The drought of March has pierced unto the root
4 And bathed each vein with liquor that has power
5 To generate therein and sire the flower;
6 When Zephyr also has, with his sweet breath,
7 Quickened again, in every holt and heath,
8 The tender shoots and buds, and the young sun
9 Into the Ram one half his course has run,
10 And many little birds make melody
11 That sleep through all the night with open eye
12 (So Nature pricks them on to ramp and rage)—
13 Then do folk long to go on pilgrimage,
14 And palmers to go seeking out strange strands,
15 To distant shrines well known in sundry lands.
16 And specially from every shire's end
17 Of England they to Canterbury wend,
18 The holy blessed martyr there to seek
19 Who help ed them when they lay so ill and weak
20 Befell that, in that season, on a day
21 In Southwark, at the Tabard, as I lay
22 Ready to start upon my pilgrimage
23 To Canterbury, full of devout **homage,**
24 There came at nightfall to that hostelry
25 Some nine and twenty in a company
26 Of **sundry** persons who had chanced to fall
27 In fellowship, and pilgrims were they all
28 That toward Canterbury town would ride.

NOTES

29 The rooms and stables spacious were and wide,

30 And well we there were eased, and of the best.

31 And briefly, when the sun had gone to rest,

32 So had I spoken with them, every one,

33 That I was of their fellowship anon,

34 And made agreement that we'd early rise

35 To take the road, as you I will **apprise.**

36 But none the less, whilst I have time and space,

37 Before yet farther in this tale I pace,

38 It seems to me accordant with reason

39 To inform you of the state of every one

40 Of all of these, as it appeared to me,

41 And who they were, and what was their degree,

42 And even how arrayed there at the inn;

43 And with a knight thus will I first begin.

FROM THE WIFE OF BATH'S TALE

44 And so befell it that this King Arthur

45 Had at his court a lusty bachelor

46 Who, on a day, came riding from river;

47 And happened that, alone as she was born,

48 He saw a maiden walking through the corn,

49 From whom, in spite of all she did and said,

50 Straightway by force he took her maidenhead;

51 For which violation was there such clamour,

52 And such appealing unto King Arthur,

53 That soon condemned was this knight to be dead

54 By course of law, and should have lost his head,

55 Peradventure, such being the statute then;

56 But that the other ladies and the queen

57 So long prayed of the king to show him grace,

58 He granted life, at last, in the law's place,

59 And gave him to the queen, as she should will,

60 Whether she'd save him, or his blood should spill.

61 The queen she thanked the king with all her might,

62 And after this, thus spoke she to the knight,

63 When she'd an opportunity, one day:

64 "You stand yet," said she, "in such poor a way

65 That for your life you've no security.

66 I'll grant you life if you can tell to me

67 What thing it is that women most desire.

68 Be wise, and keep your neck from iron dire!

69 And if you cannot tell it me anon,

70 Then will I give you license to be gone

71 A twelvemonth and a day, to search and learn
72 Sufficient answer in this grave concern.
73 And your knight's word I'll have, ere forth you pace,
74 To yield your body to me in this place."

...

75 This knight my tale is chiefly told about
76 When what he went for he could not find out,
77 That is, the thing that women love the best,
78 Most saddened was the spirit in his breast;
79 But home he goes, he could no more delay.
80 The day was come when home he turned his way;
81 And on his way it chanced that he should ride
82 In all his care, beneath a forest's side,
83 And there he saw, a-dancing him before,
84 Full four and twenty ladies, maybe more;
85 Toward which dance eagerly did he turn
86 In hope that there some wisdom he should learn.
87 But truly, ere he came upon them there,
88 The dancers vanished all, he knew not where.
89 No creature saw he that gave sign of life,
90 Save, on the greensward sitting, an old wife;
91 A fouler person could no man devise.
92 Before the knight this old wife did arise,
93 And said: "Sir knight, hence lies no travelled way.
94 Tell me what thing you seek, and by your fay.
95 Perchance you'll find it may the better be;
96 These ancient folk know many things," said she.
97 "Dear mother," said this knight assuredly,
98 "I am but dead, save I can tell, truly,
99 What thing it is that women most desire;
100 Could you inform me, I'd pay well your hire."
101 "Plight me your troth here, hand in hand," said she,
102 "That you will do, whatever it may be,
103 The thing I ask if it lie in your might;
104 And I'll give you your answer ere the night."
105 "Have here my word," said he. "That thing I grant."
106 "Then," said the crone, "of this I make my vaunt,
107 Your life is safe; and I will stand thereby,
108 Upon my life, the queen will say as I.
109 Let's see which is the proudest of them all
110 That wears upon her hair kerchief or caul,
111 Shall dare say no to that which I shall teach;
112 Let us go now and without longer speech."

113 Then whispered she a sentence in his ear,
114 And bade him to be glad and have no fear.

115 When they were come unto the court, this knight
116 Said he had kept his promise as was right,
117 And ready was his answer, as he said.
118 Full many a noble wife, and many a maid,
119 And many a widow, since they are so wise,
120 The queen herself sitting as high justice,
121 Assembled were, his answer there to hear;
122 And then the knight was bidden to appear.

123 Command was given for silence in the hall,
124 And that the knight should tell before them all
125 What thing all worldly women love the best.
126 This knight did not stand dumb, as does a beast,
127 But to this question promptly answered
128 With manly voice, so that the whole court heard

129 "My liege lady, generally," said he,
130 "Women desire to have the sovereignty
131 As well upon their husband as their love,
132 And to have mastery their man above;
133 This thing you most desire, though me you kill
134 Do as you please, I am here at your will."
135 In all the court there was no wife or maid
136 Or widow that denied the thing he said,
137 But all held, he was worthy to have life.
138 And with that word up started the old wife
139 Whom he had seen a-sitting on the green.
140 "Mercy," cried she, "my sovereign lady queen!
141 Before the court's dismissed, give me my right.
142 'Twas I who taught the answer to this knight;
143 For which he did gave his word to me, out there,
144 That the first thing I should of him require
145 He would do that, if it lay in his might.
146 Before the court, now, pray I you, sir knight,"
147 Said she, "that you will take me for your wife;
148 For well you know that I have saved your life.
149 If this be false, say nay, upon your fay!"
150 This knight replied: "Alas and welaway!
151 That I so promised I will not protest.
152 But for God's love pray make a new request.
153 Take all my wealth and let my body go."

154 "Nay then," said she, "beshrew us if I do!
155 For though I may be foul and old and poor,
156 I will not, for all metal and all ore
157 That from the earth is dug or lies above,
158 Be aught except your wife and your true love."

159 "My love?" cried he, "nay, rather my damnation!
160 Alas! that any of my race and station
161 Should ever so dishonoured foully be!"
162 But all for naught; the end was this, that he
163 Was so **constrained** he needs must go and wed,
164 And take his ancient wife and go to bed.

165 Now, peradventure, would some men say here,
166 That, of my negligence, I take no care
167 To tell you of the joy and all the array
168 That at the wedding feast were seen that day.
169 Make a brief answer to this thing I shall;
170 I say, there was no joy or feast at all;
171 There was but heaviness and grievous sorrow;
172 For privately he wedded on the morrow,
173 And all day, then, he hid him like an owl;
174 So sad he was, his old wife looked so foul.

175 Great was the woe the knight had in his thought
176 When he, with her, to marriage bed was brought;
177 He rolled about and turned him to and fro.
178 His old wife lay there, always smiling so,
179 And said: "O my dear husband, ben'cite!
180 Fares every knight with wife as you with me?
181 Is this the custom in King Arthur's house?
182 Are knights of his all so fastidious?
183 I am your own true love and, more, your wife;
184 And I am she who saved your very life;
185 And truly, since I've never done you wrong,
186 Why do you treat me so, this first night long?
187 You act as does a man who's lost his wit;
188 What is my fault? For God's love tell me it,
189 And it shall be amended, if I may."

190 "Amended!" cried this knight, "Alas, nay, nay!
191 It will not be amended ever, no!
192 You are so loathsome, and so old also,
193 And therewith of so low a race were born,
194 It's little wonder that I toss and turn.
195 Would God my heart would break within my breast!"

196   "Is this," asked she, "the cause of your unrest?"
197   "Yes, truly," said he, "and no wonder 'tis."

...

198   "Now, sir, with age you have **upbraided** me;
199   And truly, sir, though no authority
200   Were in a book, you gentles of honour
201   Say that men should the aged show favour,
202   And call him father, of your gentleness;
203   And authors could I find for this, I guess.

204   Now since you say that I am foul and old,
205   Then fear you not to be made a cuckold;
206   For dirt and age, as prosperous I may be,
207   Are mighty wardens over chastity.
208   Nevertheless, since I know your delight,
209   I'll satisfy your worldly appetite.

210   "Two choices," said she, "which one will you try,
211   To have me foul and old until I die,
212   And be to you a true and humble wife,
213   And never anger you in all my life;
214   Or else to have me young and very fair
215   And take your chance with those who will repair
216   Unto your house, and all because of me,
217   Or in some other place, as well may be.
218   Now choose which you like better and reply."

219   This knight considered, and did sorely sigh,
220   But at the last replied as you shall hear:
221   "My lady and my love, and wife so dear,
222   I put myself in your wise governing;
223   Do you choose which may be the more pleasing,
224   And bring most honour to you, and me also.
225   I care not which it be of these things two;
226   For if you like it, that suffices me."

227   "Then have I got of you the mastery,
228   Since I may choose and govern, in earnest?"
229   "Yes, truly, wife," said he, "I hold that best."

230   "Kiss me," said she, "we'll be no longer wroth,
231   For by my truth, to you I will be both;
232   That is to say, I'll be both good and fair.
233   I pray God I go mad, and so declare,

NOTES

234 If I be not to you as good and true
235 As ever wife was since the world was new.
236 And, save I be, at dawn, as fairly seen
237 As any lady, empress, or great queen
238 That is between the east and the far west,
239 Do with my life and death as you like best.
240 Throw back the curtain and see how it is."

241 And when the knight saw verily all this,
242 That she so very fair was, and young too,
243 For joy he clasped her in his strong arms two,
244 His heart bathed in a bath of utter bliss;
245 A thousand times, all in a row, he'd kiss.
246 And she obeyed his wish in everything
247 That might give pleasure to his love-liking.

248 And thus they lived unto their lives' fair end,
249 In perfect joy; and Jesus to us send
250 Meek husbands, and young ones, and fresh in bed,
251 And good luck to outlive them that we wed.
252 And I pray Jesus to cut short the lives
253 Of those who'll not be governed by their wives;
254 And old and **querulous** niggards with their pence,
255 And send them soon a mortal pestilence!

THINK QUESTIONS CA-CCSS: CA.RL.11-12.1, CA.L.11-12.4a, CA.L.11-12.4d

1. Why might the time of year that the pilgrims are traveling, as identified in the Prologue, be meaningful? Use textual evidence to support your answer.

2. An antihero is a main character who lacks traditional heroic qualities such as being noble and courageous. In what way is the knight in the Wife of Bath's tale an antihero? Refer to one or more details from the text to support your answer.

3. In what way does the last part of the Wife of Bath's tale deal with the concept of beauty? Use textual evidence to support your answer.

4. What context clues help you to determine the meaning of the word **apprise** as it is used in *The Canterbury Tales*? What do you think "apprise" might mean? Look up the meaning of "apprise" and compare the dictionary definition with your guess.

5. Use context to determine the meaning of the word **upbraided** as it is used in *The Canterbury Tales*. Explain how context helps you determine the word's meaning. Write your definition of *upbraided* here.

CLOSE READ

CA-CCSS: CA.RL.11-12.1, CA.RL.11-12.2, CA.RL.11-12.3, CA.RL.11-12.4, CA.W.11-12.4, CA.W.11-12.5, CA.W.11-12.6, CA.W.11-12.9a, CA.W.11-12.10

Reread the excerpt from the poem *The Canterbury Tales.* As you reread, complete the Focus Questions below. Then use your answers and annotations from the questions to help you complete the Writing Prompt.

 FOCUS QUESTIONS

1. Highlight a word in the Prologue to *The Canterbury Tales* that you did not know before reading the text. Then use one or more strategies to determine the word's meaning. Write the definitions of the word, describe the steps you took to learn the word's meaning, and explain how knowing the word's meaning helps you better understand the text. Use the annotation tool to write your response to these questions.

2. Chaucer uses strong modifiers to show the anger and frustration that the knight feels when he must marry the old woman. What motivates these emotions? Highlight some of these adjectives and adverbs in the seventh and eighth stanzas of the Wife of Bath's tale and write annotations to explain how they reflect the knight's unhappiness. Study context to gain a greater understanding of the words you choose.

3. One theme of the Wife of Bath's tale involves true love. What can you infer about her attitude toward true love? Highlight evidence from the text that will help support your ideas. Choose one piece of evidence from the middle of the excerpt and one from near the end.

4. Another theme of the Wife of Bath's tale involves the role of a woman's physical beauty in male-female relationships. Use textual evidence to infer what the knight's attitude is toward beauty, or the lack thereof. Highlight in the eighth and tenth stanzas and make annotations to explain your choices.

5. In the Wife of Bath's tale, what can you infer about the Wife's attitude toward the connection between people's social rank and how well they behave and how wise they are? Highlight evidence from different parts of the excerpt and make annotations to explain your choices.

6. As you reread the excerpt from the Prologue of *The Canterbury Tales*, think about how such pilgrimages to Canterbury might have contributed to national unity in medieval England. Keep in mind that, at the time, St. Thomas Becket was considered a national hero. Then apply the unit's Essential Question to the text. In *The Canterbury Tales*, where does history end and legend begin? Highlight evidence from the excerpt and make annotations to explain your response.

WRITING PROMPT

Chaucer's tales include many examples of magic and witchcraft. Think about some of the traditional qualities associated with witches in legends. How is magic used to bring about justice and redemption? Write a response in which you compare and contrast the descriptions and actions of the old woman in the Wife of Bath's tale with those of a witch. How does her "magic" redeem the knight's behavior? Use textual evidence to support your position, including inferences.

THE ONCE AND FUTURE KING

FICTION
T.H. White
1958

INTRODUCTION

T.H. White's Arthurian novel *The Once and Future King* is considered a masterpiece of modern fantasy literature. In writing the novel, White altered the source material about King Arthur to reflect on power and justice from a decidedly modern perspective. In White's version, Merlyn is an anachronistic character who has existed for centuries, living backwards in time. Merlyn uses his knowledge of future history to help shape King Arthur's ideas about "might and right."

"...now he was to see for certain whether he had lived in vain."

 FIRST READ

Excerpt from Book II Chapter VI

1   The King of England painfully climbed the two hundred and eight steps which led to Merlyn's tower room, and knocked on the door. The magician was inside, with Archimedes sitting on the back of his chair, busily trying to find the square root of minus one. He had forgotten how to do it.

2   "Merlyn," said the King, panting, "I want to talk to you."

3   He closed his book with a bang, leaped to his feet, seized his wand of lignum vitae, and rushed at Arthur as if he were trying to shoo away a stray chicken.

4   "Go away!" he shouted. "What are you doing here? What do you mean by it? Aren't you the King of England? Go away and send for me! Get out of my room! I never heard of such a thing! Go away at once and send for me!"

5   "But I am here."

6   "No, you're not," retorted the old man resourcefully. And he pushed the King out of the door, slamming it in his face.

7   "Well!" said Arthur, and he went off sadly down the two hundred and eight stairs.

8   An hour later, Merlyn presented himself in the Royal Chamber, in answer to a summons which had been delivered by a page.

9   "That's better," he said, and sat down comfortably on a carpet chest.

10 "Stand up," said Arthur, and he clapped his hands for a page to take away the seat.

11 Merlyn stood up, boiling with **indignation.** The whites of his knuckles **blanched** as he clenched them.

12 "About our conversation on the subject of **chivalry**," began the King in an airy tone.

....

13 Merlyn was immediately watching him with a sharp eye. His knobbed fingers fluttered among the stars and secret signs of his gown, but he would not help the speaker. You might say that this moment was the critical one in his career—the moment towards which he had been living backward for heaven knows how many centuries, and now he was to see for certain whether he had lived in vain.

14 "I have been thinking," said Arthur, "about Might and Right. I don't think things ought to be done because you are able to do them. I think they should be done because you ought to do them. After all, a penny is a penny in any case, however much Might is exerted on either side, to prove that it is or not. Is that plain?"

15 Nobody answered.

16 "Well, I was talking to Merlyn on the battlements one day, and he mentioned that the last battle we had—in which seven hundred kerns were killed—was not so much fun as I had thought it was. Of course, battles are not fun when you come to think about them. I mean, people ought not to be killed, ought they? It is better to be alive."

17 "Very well. But the funny thing is that Merlyn was helping me to win battles. He is still helping me, for that matter, and we hope to win the battle of Bedegraine together, when it comes off."

18 "We will," said Sir Ector, who was in the secret.

19 "That seems to me to be inconsistent. Why does he help me to fight wars, if they are bad things?"

20 There was no answer from anybody, and the King began to speak with agitation.

21 "I could only think," said he, beginning to blush, "I could only think that I—that we—that he—that he wanted me to win them for a reason."

22 He paused and looked at Merlyn, who turned his head away.

23 "The reason was—was it?—the reason was that if I could be the master of my kingdom by winning these two battles, I could stop them afterwards and then do something about the business of Might. Have I guessed? Was I right?"

24 The magician did not turn his head, and his hands lay still in his lap.

25 "I was!" exclaimed Arthur.

26 And he began talking so quickly that he could hardly keep up with himself. "You see," he said, "Might is not Right. But there is a lot of Might knocking about in this world, and something has to be done about it. It is as if people were half horrible and half nice. Perhaps they are even more than half horrible, and when they are left to themselves they run wild. You get the average baron that we see nowadays, people like Sir Bruce Sans Pitié, who simply go clod-hopping round the country dressed in steel, and doing exactly what they please, for sport. It is our Norman idea about the upper classes having a **monopoly** of power, without reference to justice. Then the horrible side gets uppermost, and there is thieving and rape and plunder and torture. The people become beasts.

27 "But, you see, Merlyn is helping me to win my two battles so that I can stop this. He wants me to put things right.

28 "Lot and Uriens and Anguish and those—they are the old world, the old-fashioned order who want to have their private will. I have got to vanquish them with their own weapons—they force it upon me, because they live by force—and then the real work will begin. This battle at Bedegraine is the preliminary, you see. It is after the battle that Merlyn is wanting me to think about."

29 Arthur paused again for comment or encouragement, but the magician's face was turned away. It was only Sir Ector, sitting next to him, who could see his eyes.

30 "Now what have I thought," said Arthur, "is this. Why can't you harness Might so that it works for Right? I know it sounds nonsense, but, I mean, you can't just say there is no such thing. The Might is there, in the bad half of people, and you can't neglect it. You can't cut it out, but you might be able to direct it, if you see what I mean, so that it was useful instead of bad."

Excerpt from Book II Chapter VIII

31 Kay looked up, with his tongue between his teeth, and remarked:

32 "By the way. You remember that argument we were having about aggression? Well, I have thought of a good reason for starting a war."

33 Merlyn froze.

34 "I would like to hear it."

35 "A good reason for starting a war is simply to have a good reason! For instance, there might be a king who had discovered a new way of life for human beings—you know, something which would be good for them. It might even be the only way of saving them from destruction. Well, if the human beings were too wicked or too stupid to accept his way, he might have to force it on them, in their own interests, by the sword."

36　The magician clenched his fists, twisted his gown into screws, and began to shake all over.

37　"Very interesting," he said in a trembling voice. "Very interesting. There was just such a man when I was young—an Austrian who invented a new way of life and convinced himself that he was the chap to make it work. He tried to **impose** his reformation by the sword, and plunged the civilized world into misery and chaos. But the thing which this fellow had overlooked, my friend, was that he had had a predecessor in the reformation business, called Jesus Christ. Perhaps we may assume that Jesus knew as much as the Austrian did about saving people. But the odd thing is that Jesus did not turn the disciples into storm troopers, burn down the Temple at Jerusalem, and fix the blame on Pontius Pilate. On the contrary, he made it clear that the business of the philosopher was to make ideas *available,* and not to impose them on people."

38　Kay looked pale but obstinate.

39　"Arthur is fighting the present war," he said, "to impose his ideas on King Lot."

Excerpted from *The Once and Future King* by T.H. White, published by the Penguin Group.

 THINK QUESTIONS　CA-CCSS: CA.RL.11-12.1, CA.L.11-12.4a, CA.L.11-12.4b

1.　What is the central conflict of the excerpt? Is it resolved over the course of the passage? If so, how? Use evidence from the text to support your interpretation.

2.　From the evidence presented in the text, how might you characterize the relationship between Merlyn and Arthur?

3.　What inference can you make about the following exchange between Arthur and Merlyn?
　　"That's better," he said, and sat down comfortably on a carpet chest.
　　"Stand up," said Arthur, and he clapped his hands for a page to take away the seat.
　　Merlyn stood up, boiling with indignation. The whites of his knuckles blanched as he clenched them.
　　"About our conversation on the subject of chivalry," began the King in an airy tone.

4.　Use context to determine the meaning of the word **monopoly** as it is used in *The Once and Future King*. Write your definition of "monopoly" here.

5.　The Latin root of the word **impose** means "to put upon." Write definitions for the following related words: impose (verb), imposition (noun), imposing (adjective), impostor (noun). Identify how the meaning of the root shifts across each word. Use a dictionary for help, if needed.

CLOSE READ CA-CCSS: CA.RL.11-12.1, CA.RL.11-12.6, CA.W.11-12.4, CA.W.11-12.5, CA.W.11-12.6, CA.W.11-12.9a, CA.W.11-12.10

Reread the excerpt from *The Once and Future King*. As you reread, complete the Focus Questions below. Then use your answers and annotations from the questions to help you complete the Writing Prompt.

 FOCUS QUESTIONS

1. As you reread the text of *The Once and Future King*, remember that description and dialogue can help readers to identify character point of view. In the first section of the excerpt from Chapter VI, what can you infer about the characters? Highlight evidence in the text and use the annotation tool to explain how the language used in the passages you've chosen reveals information about the characters.

2. The second part of the excerpt from Chapter VI begins with "the moment towards which [Merlyn] had been living backward for heaven knows how many centuries, and now he was to see for certain whether he had lived in vain" (paragraph 13). What happens during the rest of this Chapter VI excerpt? What does Merlyn do? How does his behavior compare or contrast with this strong statement about the importance of this event? Highlight sections and language from the text to support your ideas.

3. How do the exchanges between Arthur and Merlyn and between Merlyn and Kay interact to create a complex story? What evidence from the text supports your ideas? How does the author use language to distinguish the characters' points of view?

4. Use your understanding of theme, tone, connotation, biased language, point of view, and explicit versus implicit meaning to give an overview of the rhetoric used in the excerpt. Highlight evidence from the text to support your analysis.

5. The Essential Question for this unit asks, Where does history end and legend begin? Consider *The Once and Future King* not only as a work of historical fiction but also as an allegory for World War II. An allegory is a story in which the characters and events are symbols for ideas or events outside the text. Which characters, details, and events from the excerpt might allude to historical events instead of Arthurian legend? Why might the author have chosen to comment on the events of World War II in this way? Highlight textual evidence to support your response.

WRITING PROMPT

In *The Once and Future King,* the narrator indicates that Arthur's speech about Might and Right was the critical moment of Merlyn's career. Why is this event so important? Does this excerpt make clear whether Merlyn's goals are achieved? Why or why not? State your claim and use your understanding of point of view, connotation, and use of language to support your analysis. Use evidence from the text as you support your claim.

LE MORTE D'ARTHUR

FICTION
Sir Thomas Malory
1485

INTRODUCTION

In the 15th century, Sir Thomas Malory translated and organized the diverse body of existing Arthurian romance tales that had developed in England and France since Anglo-Saxon times. Malory's retelling of the heroic adventures of King Arthur and the knights of the Round Table, *Le Morte d'Arthur*, became the first prose masterpiece of the English language. In this excerpt, King Arthur engages in his final battle, waged against an army commanded by his illegitimate son, Mordred.

"The king cried out as he lay in his bed and slept, 'Help, help!'"

 FIRST READ

Part Eight: The Death of Arthur
IV: The Day of Destiny

From 3

1 Upon Trinity Sunday at night King Arthur dreamed a wonderful dream, and that was this: it seemed that he saw upon a platform a chair and the chair was fastened to a wheel; thereupon King Arthur sat in the richest cloth of gold that might be made. And the king thought that under him, far from him, was hideous deep black water; therein were all manner of serpents and worms and wild beasts, foul and horrible. Suddenly the king thought that the wheel turned upside-down and he fell among the serpents, and every beast caught him by a limb. The king cried out as he lay in his bed and slept, "Help, help!"

2 Then knights, squires, and yeomen awakened the king, and he was so dazed that he knew not where he was. He stayed awake until it was nigh day and then he fell to slumbering again, not sleeping but not thoroughly awake. Then it seemed to the king that Sir Gawain actually came unto him with a number of fair ladies.

3 When King Arthur saw him he cried, "Welcome, my sister's son; I thought that ye were dead. And now that I see thee alive, much am I beholden unto almighty Jesus. Ah, fair nephew, what are these ladies that have come hither with you?"

4 "Sir," said Sir Gawain, "all those are ladies for whom I have fought when I was a living man. And all these are those whom I did battle for in righteous quarrels; at their devout prayer, because I did battle for them righteously, God hath given them the grace to bring me hither unto you. Thus God hath given me leave to warn you away from your death: for if ye fight to-morn with Sir Mordred, as ye have both agreed, doubt ye not that ye shall be slain, and the most part of your people on both sides. Through the great grace and

goodness that almighty Jesus hath unto you, and through pity for you and many other good men who would be slain there, God in His special grace hath sent me to you to give you warning that in no wise should ye do battle to-morn; but ye should make a treaty for a month. And make this offer generously to-morn so as to assure the delay, for within a month Sir Lancelot shall come with all his noble knights and rescue you worshipfully and slay Sir Mordred and all who ever will hold with him."

5   Then Sir Gawain and all the ladies vanished; at once the king called upon his knights, squires, and yeomen and charged them quickly to fetch his noble lords and wise bishops unto him. When they had come the king told them of his vision and what Sir Gawain had said to him: that if he fought on the morn, he would be slain. Then the king commanded and charged Sir Lucan le Butler, his brother Sir Bedivere, and two bishops to make a treaty in any way for a month with Sir Mordred: "And spare not; offer him lands and goods, as much as ye think best."

6   They departed and came to Sir Mordred, where he had a grim host of a hundred thousand men. There they entreated Sir Mordred a long time, and at last it was agreed for Sir Mordred to have Cornwall and Kent during King Arthur's days and all England after the king's days.

4

7   Then they agreed that King Arthur and Sir Mordred should meet between their two hosts, and that each of them should bring fourteen persons with him. They came back with this word to King Arthur.

8   Then he said, "I am glad that this is done." So he went into the field.

9   When King Arthur prepared to depart for the meeting in the field he warned all his host that if they should see any sword drawn, "see that ye come on fiercely and slay that traitor Sir Mordred, for I in no wise trust him."

10   In like wise Sir Mordred warned his host: "If ye see any sword drawn, see that ye come on fiercely and then slay all who stand before you, for in no way will I trust this treaty; I know well that my father wishes to be avenged upon me."

11   So they met for their appointment and were thoroughly agreed and accorded; wine was fetched and they drank together. Just then an **adder** came out of a little heath-bush and stung a knight on the foot. When the knight felt the sting, he looked down and saw the adder; at once he drew his sword to slay the adder, and thought to cause no harm. But when the hosts on both sides saw that sword drawn, they blew trumpets and horns and shouted grimly, and the two hosts rushed toward each other.

NOTES

12 Then King Arthur mounted his horse and said, "Alas, this unhappy day!" So he rode to join his party, and Sir Mordred did in like wise. And never since was there seen a more **doleful** battle in any Christian land, for there was great rushing and riding, thrusting and striking, and many a grim word was spoken by each side, and many a deadly stroke was dealt. But King Arthur rode steadily throughout the army of Sir Mordred many times and did full nobly, as a noble king should; never at any time did he weaken. And Sir Mordred did his duty that day and put himself in great peril. Thus they fought all the long day, and no knight ever stinted till he was laid to the cold earth. So they fought on till it was near night, and by that time there were a hundred thousand who lay dead upon the ground. Then King Arthur was madly wroth out of measure, when he saw that so many of his people were slain. When the king looked about him he was aware that of all his host and of all his good knights no more were left alive but two: one was Sir Lucan le Butler, and the other his brother Sir Bedivere; and they were both sorely wounded.

13 "Jesus, mercy!" said the king. "Where are all my noble knights? Alas, that ever I should see this doleful day! For now I have come to my end. But would to God that I knew where that traitor Sir Mordred, who hath caused all this mischief, is."

14 Then King Arthur looked about and saw where Sir Mordred stood leaning upon his sword among a great heap of dead men. "Now give me my spear," said King Arthur to Sir Lucan, "for yonder I have spied the traitor who hath wrought all this woe."

15 "Sir, let him be," said Sir Lucan, "for he brings ill fortune, And if ye can pass through this unlucky day, ye shall be right well revenged upon him. Good lord, remember your night's dream and what the spirit of Sir Gawain told you last night. God in His great goodness hath preserved you so far. Therefore for God's sake, my lord, leave off now; for, blessed be God, ye have won the field: here we three are alive, but with Sir Mordred no one is alive. Therefore if ye leave off now, this wicked day of destiny is over."

16 "Now betide me death, betide me life," said the king, "now that I see him yonder alone, he shall never escape my hands! For I shall never have him at better avail."

17 "God speed you well!" said Sir Bedivere.

18 Then the king got his spear in both his hands and ran toward Sir Mordred, crying, "Traitor, now has thy death-day come!"

19 When Sir Mordred heard King Arthur he ran toward him with his sword drawn in his hand. Then King Arthur **smote** Sir Mordred under the shield with a

thrust of his spear on through the body more than a fathom. When Sir Mordred felt that he had his death-wound, he thrust himself with all his might up to the handguard of King Arthur's spear; and right so, holding his sword in both his hands, he smote his father King Arthur upon the side of the head so that the sword pierced the helmet and the brain-pan. Therewith Sir Mordred fell stark dead to the earth; and the noble King Arthur fell to the earth and there he **swooned** often, and Sir Lucan and Sir Bedivere lifted him up each time. So they led him, weak between them, to a little chapel not far from the sea, and when the king was there he seemed reasonably comfortable.

20 Then they heard people cry out in the field.

21 "Now go thou, Sir Lucan," said the king, "and let me know what that noise in the field betokens."

22 So Sir Lucan departed slowly, for he was grievously wounded in many places; as he went he saw and noticed by the moonlight how plunderers and robbers had come into the field to plunder and to rob many a full noble knight of brooches and beads, of many a good ring, and of many a rich jewel. And whoever was not fully dead, the robbers slew them for their armor and their riches. When Sir Lucan understood this work, he came back to the king as quickly as he could and told him all that he had heard and seen.

23 "Therefore, by my counsel," said Sir Lucan, "it is best that we bring you to some town."

5

24 "I would it could be so," said the king, "but I cannot stand, my head aches so. Ah, Sir Lancelot, this day have I sorely missed thee! And alas, that ever I was against thee! For now I have my death, whereof Sir Gawain warned me in my dream."

25 Then Sir Lucan took up the king on one side and Sir Bedivere did so on the other side, and in the lifting the king swooned. Also with the lifting, Sir Lucan fell into a swoon and part of his guts fell out of his body, and therewith the noble knight's heart burst. When the king awoke he beheld Sir Lucan, how he lay foaming at the mouth, and how part of his guts lay at his feet.

26 "Alas," said the king, "this is to me a full heavy sight to see this noble duke die so for my sake; for he wished to help me, he who had more need of help than I. Alas, he would not complain, his heart was so set upon helping me. Now Jesus have mercy upon his soul!"

27 Then Sir Bedivere wept for the death of his brother.

28   "Leave this mourning and weeping," said the king, "for all this will not avail me. For wit thou well, if I might live myself the death of Sir Lucan would grieve me evermore, but my time passeth on fast. Therefore take though here Excalibur, my good sword, and go with it to yonder water's side; when thou comest there, I charge thee to throw my sword into that water and come again and tell me what thou saw there."

29   "My lord," said Sir Bedivere, "your command shall be done, and quickly I shall bring you word back."

30   So Sir Bedivere departed. And along the way he beheld that noble sword, that the pommel and the haft were all of precious stones. Then he said to himself, "If I throw this rich sword into the water, thereof shall never come good, but only harm and loss." Then Sir Bedivere hid Excalibur under a tree, and as soon as he might he came again unto the king and said that he had been at the water and had thrown the sword into the water.

31   "What saw thou there?" said the king.

32   "Sir," he said, "I saw nothing but waves and winds."

33   "That is untruly said by thee," said the king. "Therefore go thou quickly again and do my command. As thou art dear to me, spare not but throw it in."

34   Then Sir Bedivere returned again and took the sword in his hand, and again he thought it a sin and a shame to throw away that noble sword. So once more he hid the sword and returned again and told the king that he had been at the water and done his command.

35   "What saw thou there?" said the king.

36   "Sir," he said, "I saw nothing but waves and winds."

37   "Ah, traitor untrue," said King Arthur, "now hast thou betrayed me twice! Who would have thought that thou who hast been to me so lief and dear and thou who art called a noble knight would betray me for the richness of this sword? But now go again quickly; thy long **tarrying** putteth me in great jeopardy of my life, for I have taken cold. And unless thou do now as I bid thee, if ever I may see thee again I shall slay thee with my own hands; for thou would for my rich sword see me dead."

38   Then Sir Bedivere departed and went to the sword and quickly took it up and went to the water's side, and there he bound the girdle around the hilt; then he threw the sword as far into the water as he might. And there came an arm and a hand above the water which caught it and shook and **brandished** it

thrice and then vanished with the sword into the water. So Sir Bedivere came back to the king and told him what he saw.

39   "Alas," said the king, "help me hence, for I fear that I have tarried over-long."

40   Then Sir Bedivere took the king upon his back and so went with him to the water's side. When they reached there they saw a little barge which waited fast by the bank with many fair ladies in it. Among them all was a queen, and they all had black hoods; they all wept and shrieked when they saw King Arthur.

41   "Now put me into that barge," said the king.

42   Sir Bedivere did so gently, and three queens received him there with great mourning and put him down; in one of their laps King Arthur laid his head. Then that queen said, "Ah, dear brother, why have ye tarried so long from me? Alas, this wound on your head hath caught over-much cold."

43   So they rowed from the land and Sir Bedivere beheld all those ladies go from him. Then Sir Bedivere cried, "Ah, my lord Arthur, what shall become of me, now that ye go from me and leave me here alone among my enemies?"

44   "Comfort thyself," said the king, "and do as well as thou may, for in me is no more trust to trust in. I must go into the Vale of Avalon to heal me of my grievous wound. And if thou hear nevermore of me, pray for my soul!"

45   But ever the queens and ladies wept and shrieked, so that it was a pity to hear. As soon as Sir Bedivere had lost sight of the barge, he wept and wailed and then took to the forest and walked all night. And in the morning he was aware of a chapel and a hermitage between two ancient woods.

...

From 7

46   Yet some men say in many parts of England that King Arthur is not dead, but was taken by the will of our Lord Jesus into another place. And men say that he shall come again and shall win the Holy Cross. Yet I will not say that it shall be so; rather, I would say that here in this world he changed his form of life. But many men say that there is written upon his tomb this line:

47   HERE LIES ARTHUR
THE ONCE AND FUTURE KING

THINK QUESTIONS CA-CCSS: CA.RL.11-12.1, CA.L.11-12.4a, CA.L.11-12.4d

1. At the end of the selection, the author says that King Arthur gets on a barge and goes "into the Vale of Avalon." What is really happening in this scene? How do you know? Cite textual evidence to support your inference.

2. Describe the character of King Arthur. What character traits does he show in this selection? Support your response with evidence from the text.

3. Describe the battle scene. How does the author use details to describe the fight? On what or on whom does the author focus in the scene? Cite textual evidence to support your answer.

4. Based on the meaning of the suffix -ed, which part of speech would you predict the vocabulary word **swooned** belongs to? Look for any context clues that support your response. Then explain how the suffix and the context helped you determine the part of speech.

5. Use the context clues provided in the passage to determine the meaning of **tarrying**. Write your definition of *tarrying* here. How do nearby words help to convey its meaning? Check your definition in a print or online dictionary.

CLOSE READ
CA-CCSS: CA.RL.11-12.1, CA.RL.11-12.2, CA.RL.11-12.3, CA.RL.11-12.4, CA.W.11-12.4, CA.W.11-12.5, CA.W.11-12.6, CA.W.11-12.9a, CA.W.11-12.10

Reread the excerpts from *Le Morte d'Arthur*. Then use your answers and annotations from the questions to help you complete the Writing Prompt.

FOCUS QUESTIONS

1. As you reread *Le Morte d'Arthur*, pay close attention to how the author develops the character of Arthur. What words and phrases does he use? What tone does he create with his word choices? Highlight evidence in the text and use the annotation tool to analyze the development of Arthur's character.

2. In paragraphs 6 and 7, what do Arthur and Mordred tell their hosts, or armies? What happens as a result? What impact does this event have on the rest of the plot? Make annotations to explain your response. Support your response with textual evidence.

3. King Arthur and his knights make repeated references to the Christian God and religion. What can you infer about the role of religion in England during the fifteenth century based on these references? Highlight examples of religious connections and use the annotation tool to note what these references reveal about England. Support your response with textual evidence.

4. King Arthur asks Sir Bedivere to do something three times. What does Arthur ask Sir Bedivere to do? What does Sir Bedivere do, and what is the final result? Why is this action important to Arthur, and what might it symbolize? Highlight your evidence and annotate to explain your ideas. Support your response with textual evidence.

5. At the end of the selection, what happens to Arthur? What does this ending say about Arthur's character and the Arthurian legend? How does this ending help you determine the theme? Highlight evidence from the text that will help support your ideas.

6. Recall the unit's Essential Question: Where does history end and legend begin? Which parts of *Le Morte d'Arthur* sound like history? Which sound like legend? What conclusion can you draw based on your ideas? Highlight evidence from the text to support your ideas.

WRITING PROMPT

Analyze the character of King Arthur as presented in this selection from *Le Morte d'Arthur*. What words and phrases does the author use to describe his words and actions? In what way do his actions reflect heroes from other stories? Then make a claim as to which traits make Arthur an archetypal hero. Use your understanding of story elements to build your analysis. Cite textual evidence to support your response.

CONVERSATION
WITH
GEOFFREY ASHE
RE: KING ARTHUR

NON-FICTION
Geoffrey Ashe
1999

INTRODUCTION

B ritish cultural historian Geoffrey Ashe has written numerous books and articles centering on the factual analysis of the King Arthur legend. Ashe has advanced the theory that a King Arthur figure did exist, and that Riothamus, a British military leader from the 5th century, is likely the man behind the legend. This excerpt from an interview of Ashe by Britannia.com provides insight into Ashe's historical approach to the study of Arthur.

"It may be factual. We must face the possibility that it isn't."

FIRST READ

1 *Since the twelfth century, a lot of creative effort has been expended on Arthur, and, in recent years, that creativity has taken the form of film, video, TV games, comic books, music and scholarly research. How do you account for the amazing persistence of these stories over the centuries?*

2 The versions that are most familiar, bringing in the Round Table and Merlin and Guinevere and Lancelot, took shape in medieval Europe. One reason for their becoming popular was that they appealed to a wide variety of interests, in an age when there wasn't much in the way of imaginative fiction. They offered stories of adventure and war and love and magic and religion. They had something for everybody who reads such things at all, and that included women, whose tastes in literature were becoming influential.

3 Of course that's not the whole of it. As you point out, Arthur isn't purely a medieval character. He keeps fading out and coming back, and he has been pictured differently in different periods. I think there is a constant factor that has a great deal to do with his vitality. One way or another, his legend embodies the dream of a golden age which is found in many societies and mythologies. It's a haunting, persistent dream. Even modern novelists, well aware that there never was a real golden age, have pictured Arthur's reign as a time when people of vision and courage were on top for a while, surviving against the odds, and going down gloriously. It's something we would like to believe in.

...

4 *Prior to Geoffrey of Monmouth, in the twelfth century, there were oral and written traditions concerning Arthur, but most of what we "know" of him is due to Geoffrey, who published his highly imaginative History of the Kings of Britain in the late 1130s. Without him, would we have even heard of Arthur?*

Would the subsequent developers of the story, Wace, Chretien de Troyes, Layamon, Malory, and others, have written about him? Does Geoffrey, ultimately, deserve all the credit?

5   It's always risky to guess at what would have happened if things had gone otherwise. But Arthur's fame before Geoffrey was strictly among the Welsh, Cornish and Bretons, the Celtic peoples of the west, descended from Britons of his own time or apparent time. If Geoffrey hadn't expanded the saga into a "history" that was read throughout most of Europe, it might have stayed regional and never inspired authors outside. The Irish had a hero something like Arthur, Finn MacCool, and stories of Finn spread to Scotland, but that's as far as they went. No one like Geoffrey took him up, and he never attained international renown as Arthur did.

...

6   *We know that, over the years, King Arthur has proven to be a mother lode of source material for writers and other artists, and it has been said that even some reigning English monarchs found ways to put the "King" to work for them. Can you explain?*

7   English kings during the Middle Ages definitely believed in Arthur. It was good for their morale and good for the Crown's **mystique** that they should be heirs of such a famous monarch. Practical politics were involved. Edward I claimed to rule Scotland on the ground that Arthur had ruled Scotland! Later, propagandists for the Tudor sovereigns, who were part Welsh, made much of their **alleged** Arthurian ancestry, and it enhanced the prestige of the greatest of them, Elizabeth I. Later again, Tennyson's best-selling Idylls of the King, a poetic evocation of Arthur in terms of Victorian ideals, helped to revive the glamour of the Crown when dissatisfaction with the actual Victoria had laid it open to attack.

...

8   *The evidence for Arthur before Geoffrey of Monmouth seems to consist mostly of sketchy entries in ancient chronicles, obscure battle poems, and credulity-straining episodes from various saints' lives. Shouldn't someone who had been so successful in conquest and who was the center of a glorious court have left more of a trail behind, with better documentary support?*

9   In Dark Age Britain we have to recognize various **adverse** factors, such as the loss and destruction of manuscripts by invading armies; the character of the early material, oral rather than written; the decline of learning and even literacy among the Welsh monks who might have

kept reliable records. The whole period is plunged in obscurity from the same causes. People who were certainly real and important are no better attested.

10   An old Welsh text with some historical pretensions says Arthur was the leader of a national counter offensive against encroaching Saxons and won twelve battles in widely separated parts of the country. The passage is fairly circumstantial, and there is at least something in it, since counter action did happen, sporadically over four or five decades. I think it likely that Arthur played a conspicuous part in it at some stage. But his status as a long-term supremo could be a **retroactive** promotion inspired later by the growth of his legend. It may be factual. We must face the possibility that it isn't. Insufficient data!

11   *When did Arthur actually live . . . if he did live?*

12   He's usually imagined as living in the Middle Ages, and going around in castles with knights in armour and magnificently dressed ladies. But he certainly didn't. As I said, his legend in its best known form was a medieval creation, and authors in those days didn't care about authenticity like a modern historical novelist. When they handled a traditional story they updated it, putting things in terms of their own time, irrespective of when it was supposed to have happened. This shows in art as well, in illustrations to the Bible, for instance. You'll see a painting of the angel appearing to Mary, and a window at the back looks out on a French chateau that couldn't possibly have existed in Nazareth. So, with the Arthur story, characters in a **milieu** which the authors knew quite well to be ancient were still dressed up as knights and ladies appropriate to the twelfth or thirteenth century. Neither Arthur nor any of his circle would have been like that. To answer the question, he really belongs in the late fifth century or the early sixth, a mysterious phase after Britain broke away from the Roman Empire. He may indeed have been a king, but it's hard to say what kingship amounted to.

13   *The study of Arthur seems to be becoming a literary pursuit rather than a historical one, and perhaps with some justification, given the scarcity of hard evidence. What about archaeology... do you think that can ever tell us anything about Arthur, or is it a dead end?*

14   Archaeology may never prove anything about Arthur personally. Something might turn up: his name on a memorial stone previously overlooked, or even a coin, though no British coins for the period have been found. It's probably too much to hope for. What archaeology can do, and certainly will, is tell us more about the Dark Age Britain where his legend originated. In doing so, it can shed light on the literary process itself.

NOTES

15 For instance, recent excavations have shown that Tintagel in Cornwall was a major community during the fifth century, very likely a regional centre of government. Now Geoffrey of Monmouth says a Cornish overlord had a stronghold at Tintagel, and Arthur was begotten there. Archaeology doesn't prove the story, but it does prove that Geoffrey chose an appropriate location. It points to a tradition of Tintagel's importance at the right time, an authentic tradition, which Geoffrey drew upon. He wasn't inventing irresponsibly, out of nothing. And that must affect our assessment of him. It encourages belief in a factual basis for at least some of his account, however wildly he exaggerates and fantasizes.

16 *You had something to do with the excavations at Cadbury Castle, probably the leading candidate for being the location of "King Arthur's Camelot." Could you tell us about your involvement in that project and the results?*

17 This is another case like Tintagel, where archaeology has shed light in its own way. Cadbury is a large isolated hill in Somerset. During the last centuries B.C., its summit area was inhabited, with a protection of earthwork ramparts. There was never a castle here in the medieval sense; the fortified hill itself was the "castle," as elsewhere in southern and southwest England. The Romans captured it and evicted the people.

18 A writer in the time of Henry VIII, John Leland, said this was Camelot. The Camelot of romance is a dream city which it would be futile to look for, but it has an aspect that may be significant. It's not the capital of Britain, it's Arthur's personal headquarters. Cadbury could have become the headquarters of a real Arthur, and a dim recollection of that reality could have conjured up the fiction.

19 Believing there was evidence to support such a view, Dr. Ralegh Radford, the pioneer of British Dark Age archaeology, formed an excavation committee with Leslie Alcock as director and myself as secretary. We carried out work in 1966–70 which showed, among much else, that the hill was re-occupied in the latter part of the fifth century and refortified on a massive scale, with a new encircling rampart of stone and timber and a gate house. Whoever was in charge was clearly a chief or king with impressive resources of manpower, at any rate an "Arthur-type figure," as Alcock put it. No complete parallel for the Cadbury fortification has been found anywhere else in post-Roman Britain. It remains special and unique.

20 When Leland picked out this hill as Camelot, he picked what seems to be the most plausible candidate (as, by the way, several novelists have agreed). How did he do it? Even a modern archaeologist couldn't have

guessed that the fifth century fortification was there, embedded in the old earthworks, just by looking without digging. I would say there must have been a tradition about the hill and its powerful overlord, handed down from the Dark Ages. The overlord may have been Arthur or he may not, but as at Tintagel, archaeology shows that people who spoke of Arthur here were not talking in a void. They knew something.

21 In the film of the musical *Camelot,* you have a brief glimpse of a map of Britain, and Camelot is in Somerset. It's there because I told Warner Brothers to put it there. That is my one contribution to Hollywood.

22 *There have been various attempts to identify Arthur with someone who is well-documented. Some investigators have argued that he was a Scottish prince, others, that he was a minor Welsh king. Still others have claimed that Arthur is elusive only because he has been improperly dated, and that he is "really" Caratacus, the first century leader of British resistance to Rome, or Lucius Artorius Castus, a Roman commander of the second century. Do any of these identifications appeal to you?*

23 As full identifications, no. They tend to cancel each other out. But the Arthur of legend may well be a composite, a superhero created by **grafting** deeds of other men on to the saga of the original, and some of these figures may have gone into the making of him. That might account for Arthurian echoes which their advocates have detected. And I suspect that the basic idea is sound, only they haven't looked in the right place.

24 *Ambrosius Aurelianus, a genuine, historical character who flourished at about the right time, was a heroic figure who could be a credible original for Arthur. What disqualifies him from consideration?*

25 Nothing absolutely disqualifies him. But why should storytellers have invented another name for him when he had a perfectly good one? Early authors are quite clear that Arthur and Ambrosius were different people.

26 *That brings us to the next question. In April 1981, you published an article in Speculum, the journal of the Medieval Academy of America, in which you detailed the research that you did to identify a genuine historical figure of Arthur, who fits all the known facts. Could you summarize your conclusions as presented in that article?*

27 The discussion has gone further since 1981. You can follow it in my book *The Discovery of King Arthur* and in various articles. My new idea was to scrutinize Arthur's foreign warfare in Geoffrey of Monmouth and take it seriously. Historians had assumed that any original Arthur would never have gone outside Britain: in that respect, Geoffrey's narrative was pure fancy, and it was useless looking for clues overseas. I did look overseas

and found trustworthy records of a "king of the Britons" who took an army to Gaul toward the year 470. We even have a letter to him. He is referred to as Riothamus, which means "supreme king" or "supremely royal" and may be a sort of honorific applied to a man who had another name. His career seems to underlie at least a major portion of Geoffrey's account, and passages in a Breton text and several chronicles suggest that he was in fact the original Arthur. One or two previous writers have thought the same.

Excerpted from *Conversation with Geoffrey Ashe re: King Arthur* by Geoffrey Ashe and britannia.com, published by britannia.com.

THINK QUESTIONS   CA-CCSS: CA.RI.11-12.1, CA.L.11-12.4a, CA.L.11-12.4d

1. According to Geoffrey Ashe, why did the Arthurian legends become popular? Why do people continue to tell them? Cite textual evidence to support your response.

2. Who does Geoffrey Ashe credit for the Arthurian story gaining popularity outside of Britain? What is his response to the interviewer's question about the lack of solid evidence surrounding Arthur? Support your response with evidence from the text.

3. What contributions can archaeology make to the study of Arthur? What contributions have Geoffrey Ashe and his colleagues made? Cite textual evidence to support your answer.

4. Identify context clues in the text that suggests the meaning of the word **adverse** as it is used in "Conversation with Geoffrey Ashe." Using those context clues, write your definition of adverse here.

5. Use the context clues provided in the passage to determine the meaning of **retroactive.** Write your definition of retroactive here. Then check your definition in a print or online dictionary and write the dictionary definition below.

CLOSE READ CA-CCSS: CA.RI.11-12.1, CA.RI.11-12.2, CA.RI.11-12.3, CA.W.11-12.4, CA.W.11-12.5, CA.W.11-12.6, CA.W.11-12.9b, CA.W.11-12.10

Reread the excerpt from "Conversation with Geoffrey Ashe re: King Arthur." As you reread, complete the Focus Questions below. Then use your answers and annotations from the questions to help you complete the Writing Prompt.

 FOCUS QUESTIONS

1. What role did King Arthur play in the Middle Ages? Consider what Geoffrey Ashe says about both English people and Europe as a whole. Highlight evidence in the text and use the annotation tool to analyze how Ashe explains Arthur's role. Support your answer with textual evidence.

2. In the fourth question, the interviewer implies that a real person would have more records than Arthur does. How does Ashe respond to this question? How does this lack of information contribute to the medieval ideas about Arthur that are discussed in the answer to the fifth question? Highlight evidence to support your ideas and write annotations to explain your choices. Support your answer with textual evidence.

3. After discussing Arthur as a literary creation, the interview switches to discussing archaeology. How does Ashe support this switch? How is Ashe's archaeological work related to his answer to the fourth question? Highlight your evidence and annotate to explain your ideas. Support your answer with textual evidence.

4. Examine the historical figures mentioned by the interviewer and Ashe. What do they have in common? What does Ashe think of each suggestion of the figures as "real" Arthurs? How do these figures continue to develop Ashe's central idea? Highlight evidence from the text that will help support your ideas.

5. How does Ashe's work at Cadbury Castle support his ideas about history and Arthur? Based on that work, what answer would Ashe likely give to the unit's Essential Question: Where does history end and legend begin? Support your answer with textual evidence.

WRITING PROMPT

Analyze the development of Geoffrey Ashe's ideas as presented in this interview. How does he introduce his ideas? What is the role of the interviewer in the building of ideas? What support does Ashe offer and how does he build his central idea over the course of the interview? Use your understanding of informational text elements as you write your response. Support your writing with evidence from the text.

UNSOLVED MYSTERIES OF HISTORY:

AN EYE-OPENING INVESTIGATION INTO THE MOST BAFFLING EVENTS OF ALL TIME

NON-FICTION

Paul Aron

2000

INTRODUCTION

Author Paul Aron has said that "history makes for great detective stories." This excerpt from his book *Unsolved Mysteries of Histories* traces evidence of King Arthur throughout history and explains how various historical chronicles and literary works contributed to the King Arthur legend.

"...there weren't as many kingdoms in the world as Geoffrey had Arthur conquering."

FIRST READ

NOTES

Excerpt from Chapter 8: Who Was King Arthur?

1   The legend of King Arthur—in stark contrast to the actual man—is easy to track back to its origins. Much of the credit goes to an obscure Welsh **cleric** named Geoffrey of Monmouth, who taught at Oxford during the first half of the twelfth century. In about 1138 Geoffrey produced *The History of the Kings of Britain.*

2   The story, as Geoffrey tells it, moves toward its climax in the fifth century. **Heathen** Saxons, led by the brothers Hengist and Horsa, have invaded and destroyed much of the country. A young wizard, Merlin, arrives on the scene with prophecies of a king who will save Britain.

3   Meanwhile, King Uther falls hopelessly in love with Ygerna. Unfortunately, she's already married—to Gorlois, the duke of Cornwall. Merlin steps in to help out. He transforms Uther into an exact likeness of Gorlois, so the king can slip by the duke's guards and sleep with Ygerna. Thus is Arthur conceived.

4   Fast forward about fifteen years, when the young Arthur ascends to the throne. He routs the Saxons, confining them to a small section of Britain. Later he conquers the Picts, the Scots, the Irish, and among many others, the Icelanders. When Roman ambassadors demand he pay tribute to the emperor, Arthur crosses the English Channel and defeats their armies in France.

5   While Arthur is abroad, his nephew, Mordred, crowns himself king and lives in adultery with Arthur's queen, Guinevere. Arthur returns and slays the traitor but is himself seriously wounded. He's last seen as he's carried off to the "isle of Avalon."

6   So goes the tale, as told by Geoffrey of Monmouth. Arthur's victory is only temporary, since the Anglo-Saxons eventually do conquer Arthur's Britons

(thus making Britain into Angle-land, or England). But this only added to the story's appeal to the Britons, who yearned for a return to a golden age when they ruled the land. For them, Arthur was not dead; he was waiting for the right moment to return from Avalon.

7   That yearned-for golden age became even more golden in the imaginations of later medieval writers, who enhanced Geoffrey's legend. The French author Robert Wace introduced the Round Table, so that Arthur's knights could sit as equals. Another Frenchman, Chretien de Troyes, brought to the fore Lancelot, Arthur's loyal knight (and Guinevere's passionate lover). The German Wolfram von Eschenbach added Parzival. By the end of the Middle Ages, Arthur's fifth-century foot soldiers had become knights on horses; his fortified hills had become grand castles; and his court had become Camelot, a chivalric **utopia.**

8   It was an Englishman, Thomas Malory, whose fifteenth-century *Morte d'Arthur* combined all these elements, giving his countrymen a mythic tradition to match any nation's. There was a certain irony to this, since the original story pitted Arthur's Britons against the Anglo-Saxon ancestors of the English, but such is the nature of classic myths. They can **transcend** almost any sort of border; witness the revival of the legend in the twentieth century in variations ranging from the feminist (most notably, in the novels of Marion Zimmer Bradley) to the musical (starring Richard Burton, in the Broadway version).

9   The yearning for a return to a golden age, it seems, is eternal. When journalist Theodore H. White, quoting from the musical, referred to the Kennedy years as "one brief, shining moment," the president's administration was quickly labeled "Camelot."

10 Yet lost amid his legend was Arthur himself. Even in Geoffrey of Monmouth's own lifetime, it was clear that his *History* was anything but. In about 1197, William of Newburgh called Geoffrey's work a "laughable web of fiction" and calculated that there weren't as many kingdoms in the world as Geoffrey had Arthur conquering.

11 Since then, historians following in William's footsteps have attempted to sift from the legend the "historical" Arthur—if, indeed, he really existed.

12 Above all, that meant turning to the (very few) sources that preceded Geoffrey of Monmouth and were thus both closer to Arthur's time and less likely to have been corrupted by later mythologizing. These were mostly Welsh writings, since it was the Welsh who were descendants of the ancient Britons.

13 These Britons came to power after the fall of the Roman Empire, early in the fifth century. They had wielded considerable power under the empire, so it seemed natural (to them) that they take over after the Roman legions left.

That was unlike other areas of the former empire, where the invaders who drove out the Romans seized power. Independent Britain was therefore still in many ways Roman; the Britons, or at least their upper class, saw themselves as the heirs to the imperial culture and civilization.

14　Unfortunately for them, they also inherited the Roman enemies. The Britons immediately found themselves under attack from groups they thought of as barbarians: the Irish from the west, the Picts from the north, and the Anglo-Saxons from across the North Sea. The invaders saw no reason to withdraw just because the Britons had replaced the Romans.

15　The situation the Welsh bards described was desperate—every bit as much as that faced by the British in Geoffrey of Monmouth's account. But if we can believe a Welsh monk named Gildas, in about the year 500 the Britons won a great victory at a spot called Mount Badon. In *The Ruin of Britain,* written only about fifty years after that, Gildas described the battle and the two generations of relative peace and prosperity that followed.

16　Was this **interregnum** of Gildas the brief, shining moment of Camelot? Perhaps. But, as skeptics have been quick to point out, nowhere does Gildas mention the name of Arthur. Frustratingly, Gildas never says who commanded the Britons.

17　This was left to Nennius, another Welsh cleric. In the *History of the Britons,* which Nennius compiled sometime early in the ninth century, there's no doubt about the identity of the hero: it is "the warrior Arthur." According to Nennius, Arthur defeated the Saxons in twelve battles, at one point slaying 960 of the enemy in a single charge.

18　But can Nennius be trusted? Such obviously impossible deeds as single-handedly killing 960 of the enemy clearly belong to the traditions of epic poetry, not history. His **notoriously** disorganized material didn't help, either; the cleric himself described his approach as "making one heap" of all he found. Some historians found comfort in that, arguing that someone unable to organize anything probably also couldn't invent anything, but others just found it frustrating.

19　Welsh writers who followed Nennius also credited Arthur with the victory at Mount Badon. But, like Nennius, they were all writing at least three hundred years after the actual events. It was impossible to tell whether the oral tradition they recounted was the actual history of fifth-century Britain.

Excerpted from Unsolved Mysteries of History: An Eye-Opening Investigation into the Most Baffling Events of All Time by Paul Aron, published by John Wiley & Sons.

THINK QUESTIONS   CA-CCSS: CA.RI.11-12.1, CA.L.11-12.4a, CA.L.11-12.4d

1. The author refers to Welsh and British people and histories in the text. What is the historic relationship between the Welsh and the British? Who wrote the early histories of Arthur and why did the written accounts differ so widely? Cite textual evidence to support your answer.

2. What main question is the author trying to answer with this text? How does he try to answer that question? Does he come to a conclusion? Support your answer with evidence from the text.

3. Who does the author cite as sources in this excerpt? Why did he choose to cite these people? Support your response with evidence from the text.

4. Use context to determine the meaning of the word **transcend** as it is used in *Unsolved Mysteries of History*. Write your definition of transcend here.

5. Use context to determine the meaning of the word **interregnum** as it is used in *Unsolved Mysteries of History*. Write your definition of "interregnum" here.

CLOSE READ

CA-CCSS: CA.RI.11-12.1, CA.RI.11-12.2, CA.RI.11-12.7, CA.W.11-12.4, CA.W.11-12.5, CA.W.11-12.6, CA.W.11-12.9b, CA.W.11-12.10

Reread the excerpt from *Unsolved Mysteries of History*. As you reread, complete the Focus Questions below. Then use your answers and annotations from the questions to help you complete the Writing Prompt.

FOCUS QUESTIONS

1. Reread the text and focus on the Arthurian writers named by the author. What do almost all of them have in common? What did each contribute to the Arthurian legend? What inference can you draw about the time period based on this information? Highlight textual evidence to support your response.

2. In paragraph 7, the author mentions non-British writers. What do these writers have to do with the Arthurian legend? What inference can you draw about the legends based on this information? Write your inference using the annotation tool and highlight textual evidence to support your inference.

3. Reread Geoffrey of Monmouth's version of the Arthurian legend. In which way is this story similar to the stories you've read in this unit? In which way is it different? What does that tell you about the legend? Highlight your evidence and make annotations to explain your choices.

4. Using the annotations you've done so far, what inference can you draw about history in the time of the Britons and Anglo-Saxons? Highlight evidence from the text that supports your inference.

5. How much of the story of King Arthur as relayed by Aron is legend, and how much is history? How do you know? Highlight evidence from the text that supports your ideas.

WRITING PROMPT

What conclusion about early British history and literature can you draw based on the information presented in *Unsolved Mysteries of History*? In what way does this conclusion enhance or enrich your understanding of the Arthurian legend and its origins? Support your response with textual evidence.

THE LORD OF THE RINGS

FICTION
J.R.R. Tolkien
1954

INTRODUCTION

J. R. R. Tolkien's epic trilogy tells a classic tale of good versus evil played out in the world of Middle-earth, a setting strongly influenced by Tolkien's familiarity with Anglo-Saxon mythology. In this excerpt from the first book, "The Fellowship of the Ring," the wizard Gandalf is explaining the history of a ring that has come into the possession of the young hobbit Frodo Baggins. Crafted by the evil wizard, Sauron, as the most powerful of nine series of rings, it has had several owners, including the murderous Gollum and Frodo's adoptive elder cousin, Bilbo Baggins. Now the forces of evil are determined to get it back, which would have devastating consequences for hobbits, elves, dwarves, and humans alike.

"Many that live deserve death. And some that die deserve life."

FIRST READ

Excerpt from The Fellowship of the Ring
Book One, Chapter II: The Shadow of the Past

1   "[The Enemy] knows that it is not one of the Seven, or the Nine, for they are accounted for. He knows that it is the One. And he has at last heard, I think, of *hobbits* and the Shire.

2   "The Shire— he may be seeking for it now, if he has not already found out where it lies. Indeed, Frodo, I fear that he may even think that the long-unnoticed name of *Baggins* has become important."

3   "But this is terrible!" cried Frodo. "Far worse than the worst that I imagined from your hints and warnings. O Gandalf, best of friends, what am I to do? For now I am really afraid. What am I to do? What a pity that Bilbo did not stab that vile creature, when he had a chance!"

4   "Pity? It was Pity that **stayed** his hand. Pity, and Mercy: not to strike without need. And he has been well rewarded, Frodo. Be sure that he took so little hurt from the evil, and escaped in the end, because he began his ownership of the Ring so. With Pity."

5   "I am sorry," said Frodo. "But I am frightened; and I do not feel any pity for Gollum."

6   "You have not seen him," Gandalf broke in.

7   "No, and I don't want to," said Frodo. "I can't understand you. Do you mean to say that you, and the Elves, have let him live on after all those horrible deeds? Now at any rate he is as bad as an Orc, and just an enemy. He deserves death."

NOTES

8   "Deserves it! I daresay he does. Many that live deserve death. And some that die deserve life. Can you give it to them? Then do not be too eager to deal out death in judgment. For even the very wise cannot see all ends. I have not much hope that Gollum can be cured before he dies, but there is a chance of it. And he is bound up with the fate of the Ring. My heart tells me that he has some part to play yet, for good or ill, before the end; and when that comes, the pity of Bilbo may rule the fate of many, yours not least. In any case we did not kill him: he is very old and very wretched. The Wood-elves have him in prison, but they treat him with such kindness as they can find in their wise hearts."

9   "All the same," said Frodo, "even if Bilbo could not kill Gollum, I wish he had not kept the Ring. I wish he had never found it, and that I had not got it! Why did you let me keep it? Why didn't you make me throw it away, or, or destroy it?"

10 "Let you? Make you?" said the wizard. "Haven't you been listening to all that I have said? You are not thinking of what you are saying. But as for throwing it away, that was obviously wrong. These Rings have a way of being found. In evil hands it might have done great evil. Worst of all, it might have fallen into the hands of the Enemy. Indeed it certainly would; for this is the One, and he is exerting all his power to find it or draw it to himself.

11 "Of course, my dear Frodo, it was dangerous for you; and that has troubled me deeply. But there was so much at stake that I had to take some risk, though even when I was far away there has never been a day when the Shire has not been guarded by watchful eyes. As long as you never used it, I did not think that the Ring would have any lasting effect on you, not for evil, not at any rate for a very long time. And you must remember that nine years ago, when I last saw you, I still knew little for certain."

12 "But why not destroy it, as you say should have been done long ago?" cried Frodo again. "If you had warned me, or even sent me a message, I would have done away with it."

13 "Would you? How would you do that? Have you ever tried?"

14 "No. But I suppose one could hammer it or melt it."

15 "Try!" said Gandalf. "Try now!"

16 Frodo drew the Ring out of his pocket again and looked at it. It now appeared plain and smooth, without mark or device that he could see. The gold looked very fair and pure, and Frodo thought how rich and beautiful was its colour, how perfect was its roundness. It was an admirable thing and altogether precious. When he took it out he had intended to fling it from him into the very

hottest part of the fire. But he found now that he could not do so, not without a great struggle. He weighed the Ring in his hand, hesitating, and forcing himself to remember all that Gandalf had told him; and then with an effort of will he made a movement, as if to cast it away, but he found that he had put it back in his pocket.

17 Gandalf laughed grimly. "You see? Already you too, Frodo, cannot easily let it go, nor will to damage it. And I could not 'make' you, except by force, which would break your mind. But as for breaking the Ring, force is useless. Even if you took it and struck it with a heavy sledge-hammer, it would make no dent in it. It cannot be unmade by your hands, or by mine.

18 "Your small fire, of course, would not melt even ordinary gold. This Ring has already passed through it **unscathed,** and even unheated. But there is no smith's **forge** in this Shire that could change it at all. Not even the anvils and furnaces of the Dwarves could do that. It has been said that dragon-fire could melt and consume the Rings of Power, but there is not now any dragon left on earth in which the old fire is hot enough; nor was there ever any dragon, not even Ancalagon the Black, who could have harmed the One Ring, the Ruling Ring, for that was made by Sauron himself. There is only one way: to find the Cracks of Doom in the depths of Orodruin, the Fire-mountain, and cast the Ring in there, if you really wish to destroy it, to put it beyond the grasp of the Enemy for ever."

19 "I do really wish to destroy it!" cried Frodo. "Or, well, to have it destroyed. I am not made for **perilous** quests. I wish I had never seen the Ring! Why did it come to me? Why was I chosen?"

20 "Such questions cannot be answered," said Gandalf. "You may be sure that it was not for any merit that others do not possess: not for power or wisdom, at any rate. But you have been chosen, and you must therefore use such strength and heart and wits as you have."

21 "But I have so little of any of these things! You are wise and powerful. Will you not take the Ring?"

22 "No!" cried Gandalf, springing to his feet. "With that power I should have power too great and terrible. And over me the Ring would gain a power still greater and more deadly." His eyes flashed and his face was lit as by a fire within. "Do not tempt me! For I do not wish to become like the Dark Lord himself. Yet the way of the Ring to my heart is by pity, pity for weakness and the desire of strength to do good. Do not tempt me! I dare not take it, not even to keep it safe, unused. The wish to **wield** it would be too great, for my strength. I shall have such need of it. Great perils lie before me."

23　He went to the window and drew aside the curtains and the shutters. Sunlight streamed back again into the room. Sam passed along the path outside whistling. "And now," said the wizard, turning back to Frodo, "the decision lies with you. But I will always help you." He laid his hand on Frodo's shoulder. "I will help you bear this burden, as long as it is yours to bear. But we must do something, soon. The Enemy is moving."

Excerpted from The Lord of the Rings *by J. R. R. Tolkien, published by Houghton Mifflin Company.*

THINK QUESTIONS CA-CCSS: CA.RL.11-12.1, CA.L.11-12.4d

1. Provide three pieces of textual evidence that show Frodo and Gandalf are living in an imaginary world and not the real world.

2. Provide two pieces of textual evidence showing that Frodo is in danger.

3. What evidence can you find to support the inference that the hobbit, Frodo, is similar to a human being?

4. Remembering that the Middle English prefix *un-* means "not," use the context clues provided in the passage to determine the meaning of **unscathed**. Write your definition of *unscathed* here.

5. Remembering that the Latin suffix *-ous* means "full of," use the context clues provided in the passage to determine the meaning of **perilous**. Write your definition of "perilous" here. Then look up the meaning of "perilous" and compare the dictionary definition with your guess.

CLOSE READ   CA-CCSS: CA.RL.11-12.1, CA.RL.11-12.2, CA.RL.11-12.3, CA.RL.11-12.4, CA.W.11-12.3a, CA.W.11-12.3b, CA.W.11-12.4, CA.W.11-12.5, CA.W.11-12.6, CA.W.11-12.9a, CA.W.11-12.10

Reread the excerpt from *The Lord of the Rings*. As you reread, complete the Focus Questions below. Then use your answers and annotations from the questions to help you complete the Writing Prompt.

 FOCUS QUESTIONS

1. As you reread the text of *The Lord of the Rings*, remember that the excerpt consists of a conversation between Frodo and Gandalf. Readers have to use inference to gather details about the setting. In the first two paragraphs of the excerpt, why can you infer that the Shire is a place?

2. Middle-earth is a place that bears some similarities to the real world. What evidence is there in the third and fourth paragraphs that some of the creatures in Middle-earth have humanlike qualities?

3. Tolkien enriches his story with figurative language. In paragraph 8, what poetic device does he use in the first six sentences? Use the annotation tool to show examples. How does the use of this poetic device give weight to what Gandalf says about Gollum?

4. Paragraph 18 mentions the Cracks of Doom. Make an inference about what kind of place this is, and provide textual evidence to support this inference.

5. Recall the Essential Question for the unit: Where does history end and legend begin? Tolkien's *The Lord of the Rings* is a timeless fantasy, but it has themes that can be applied to the real world. Identify such a theme that relates to the real world and explain how Tolkien uses fantastic elements to develop it. Highlight textual evidence from the excerpt to support your response.

WRITING PROMPT

Think about how the conversation between Frodo and Gandalf provides you with information about the setting of the first part of *The Lord of the Rings*. Imagine that the next morning Frodo panics and flings the ring out his window. Write a short narrative summarizing what happens the next day. Include details describing the Shire and the creatures there based on textual evidence from the selection. Also include figurative language in your narrative.

DC COMICS:

SIXTY YEARS OF THE WORLD'S FAVORITE COMIC BOOK HEROES

NON-FICTION
Les Daniels
1995

INTRODUCTION

In the late 1930's, DC Comics introduced Superman and Batman, ushering in a new era of superheroes in American popular culture. Competitors immediately followed suit with their own comic book heroes—such as Wonder Man, Captain Marvel, Captain America, The Human Torch, Sub-Mariner, Plasticman, Blackhawk, and Blue Beetle—launching what became known as the Golden Age of Comics.

"...publishers large and small were flooding the newsstands with a cascade of costumed characters."

 FIRST READ

 NOTES

DC Inspires a Horde of Heroes

1   By 1939, the double-barreled triumph of Superman and Batman had knocked the infant comic book industry on its ear. The idea that heroes nobody had heard of a few months before could suddenly sell hundreds of thousands of copies was just too tempting to resist, and before long publishers large and small were flooding the newsstands with a cascade of costumed characters. DC had established a new genre with its super heroes, and the competition would be fast and furious.

2   A rival might come from anywhere, even the same building. Victor Fox, an accountant for DC, saw the sales figures and promptly opened his own office just a few floors away. He hired Will Eisner, later one of the most respected talents in comics, to write and draw a deliberate imitation of Superman called Wonder Man for *Wonder Comics* (May 1939). Eisner never suspected this might be illegal, but DC did and promptly sued Fox for **plagiarism.** "We beat him," says DC's Jack Liebowitz, but Fox didn't even wait for the 1940 judgment and canceled Wonder Man after his first appearance. Fox had some success later in 1939 with Blue Beetle, who got his strength from vitamins.

3   Considerably more creativity was shown in the first issue of *Marvel Comics* (October 1939), which later gave its name to its fledgling publisher. Deriving their powers respectively from fire and water, the Human Torch and the Sub-Mariner were guys with a gimmick. From the same firm in 1941 came the patriotic Captain America, created by Joe Simon and Jack Kirby; after a dispute with the publisher, the innovative team went to work at DC in 1942.

4   The toughest competitor of all was Captain Marvel, who got his start in *Whiz Comics* (February 1940). The product of a large, established firm called Fawcett Publications, Captain Marvel in his heyday was the biggest seller in the business, but in some ways he seemed suspiciously close to Superman. DC decided to sue. "It took a long time," says Jack Liebowitz. The legal battle

NOTES

dragged on for years as the two corporations duked it out like super heroes, and the dust didn't settle until 1953. DC editor Jack Schiff compiled a scrapbook documenting similarities, but the district court dismissed DC's complaint. DC appealed, and the case was heard by no less a jurist than Judge Learned Hand, who reversed the dismissal and **remanded** the case back to the lower court. At this point Fawcett finally decided to settle, and agreed to stop publishing Captain Marvel.

5   For all of that, Captain Marvel is a great character. Created by artist C. C. Beck and writer Bill Parker, the scripts developed a humorous slant in scripts provided by Otto Binder. The often **obtuse** hero was a "Big Red Cheese" to his brilliant enemy Dr. Sivana, and was nearly defeated by an intellectually advanced earthworm called Mr. Mind. Beck's simple artwork had real appeal, and kids loved the idea that young Billy Batson could turn into the "World's Mightiest Mortal" simply by uttering the magic word "Shazam!" In 1973, events came full circle when DC acquired the rights from Fawcett to revive the character with a comic book called *Shazam!*, and a successful TV series followed in 1974.

6   Captain Marvel wasn't the only hero who eventually became part of the DC family after getting his start elsewhere. When the Quality Comics Group folded during an industry slump in 1956, DC picked up two major features that had first appeared in August 1941: Plastic Man and Blackhawk. The bizarre brainchild of cartoonist Jack Cole, Plastic Man got some acid in an open wound and ended up "stretchin' like a rubber band." Cole had a surreal imagination and the convoluted **contortions** of his character were a joy to behold. Decked out in dark goggles, Plastic Man was perhaps the hippest hero in comics. All his counterparts had jealously guarded secret identities, but "Plas," a reformed criminal, just couldn't be bothered; his sidekick wasn't a kid, but a fat guy in a polka dot shirt. There has never been a funnier crime-fighter.

7   Blackhawk, by contrast, was born on the bloody battlefields of World War II. A Polish flier shot down by the Nazis, he established a **guerrilla** unit on an uninhabited island and recruited six aviators from allied nations: Andre, Chuck, Chop Chop, Olaf, Stanislaus, and Hendrickson. They had no special powers, but they did have matching uniforms and great planes. One of the first hero teams in comics, the Blackhawks flourished even after the war ended. Created by the prolific Will Eisner, the series would later benefit from the impeccable draftsmanship of Red Crandall. It began a long run at DC in 1957.

8   The acquisition over the years of characters like Captain Marvel, Plastic Man and Blackhawk strengthened DC's stable, and confirmed the company's status as the home of the most famous super heroes in the world.

Excerpted from *DC Comics: Sixty Years of the World's Favorite Comic Book Heroes* by Les Daniels, published by Bullfinch.

 THINK QUESTIONS   CA-CCSS: CA.RI.11-12.1, CA.L.11-12.4a

1. Describe two competitors to DC Comics in the late 1930s-early 1940s. How did DC Comics respond to these new companies? Cite textual evidence to support your response.

2. Who was Captain Marvel? What happened to the character and why? Support your response with evidence from the text.

3. Which two popular heroes were revived by DC Comics when Quality Comics Group folded? Compare and contrast the two heroes. Support your comparison with evidence from the text.

4. Use context to determine the meaning of the word **plagiarism** as it is used in *DC Comics: Sixty Years of the World's Favorite Comic Book Heroes*. Write your definition of *plagiarism* here.

5. Use context to determine the meaning of **contortions**. Imagining the character of Plastic Man may help. Write your definition of *contortions* here.

CLOSE READ CA-CCSS: CA.RI.11-12.1, CA.RI.11-12.3, CA.W.11-12.4, CA.W.11-12.5, CA.W.11-12.6, CA.W.11-12.9b, CA.W.11-12.10

Reread the excerpt from *DC Comics: Sixty Years of the World's Favorite Comic Book Heroes*. As you reread, complete the Focus Questions below. Then use your answers and annotations from the questions to help you complete the Writing Prompt.

FOCUS QUESTIONS

1. According to the author, what events launched the demand for superheroes? How did the comic book industry respond? Highlight evidence in the text and use the annotation tool to note the relationship between the events you highlighted.

2. In paragraph 4, the author introduces Captain Marvel. Who was this character and how was he related to DC Comics? How did DC respond to Captain Marvel, and what was the ultimate result? Highlight your evidence and annotate to explain your ideas.

3. What conclusion can you draw about DC Comics in the middle of the twentieth century based on their response to Wonder Man and Captain Marvel? What does that conclusion tell you about comic books at the time in general? Highlight your evidence and annotate to explain your ideas.

4. What was DC Comics's response to other comics companies going out of business? In what two ways did this help DC Comics? Highlight your evidence and make annotations to explain your choices.

5. Recall the unit's Essential Question: Where does history end and legend begin? How did comic book creators draw on history in the middle of the 20th century to create new superheroes? Support your response with evidence from the text.

WRITING PROMPT

Analyze the author's choices regarding the sequence of events. How does the author present the events in this history of a comic book company? Does the structure effectively convey the relationships between the events described? Why or why not? Use your understanding of signal words and phrases to support your response. Cite textual evidence to support your analysis.

THE LEGEND OF CARMAN

English Language
Development

FICTION

INTRODUCTION

This short story revisits an ancient Irish myth about an Athenian sorceress named Carman and her three sons—Dub, Dother, and Dian. Once Carman sees the fertile green fields of Ireland, she decides to conquer the current rulers, the Tuatha Dé Dannan, and make the land her home, but her sons' bad behavior leads to unforeseen complications.

"'Soon,' she cooed to the terrible trio, 'all you see will be ours.'"

NOTES

FIRST READ

1   Hearken! Attend the tale of noble Carman, the fair. Hold your tongues, and listen closely to her sorrowful story.

2   Carman, the raven-haired warrior woman from Athens, was a wonder. The gods blessed this battle-tested beauty with magic powers. Her three sons, a rank of rapacious offspring, were with her always. Dub, the Black-Hearted, had a soul as dark and empty as the deepest cavern. Dother, the Evil, hated everything. Dian, the Violent, was a walking nightmare, leaving a bevy of victims wherever he traveled. Carman and her sons had been sailing in search of land to conquer when she heard news of skirmishes on the shores of Ireland. Despite her great gifts, she never could have guessed that their next voyage would be her last. Not even her most skillful spell could save her from her sons' selfish mistake.

3   The Tuatha Dé Dannan had recently descended upon Ireland's emerald shores. Their name means "tribe of the gods," and gods they were. The Tuatha Dé Dannan came to the coast of Connemara in clouds of mist. Some say they sailed into the harbor like men and burned their boats, creating smoke that spread out across the land. Others swear that they came down from the heavens on dark clouds like a fine rain that soaked the ground. It is believed that these supernatural beings brought with them three days and three nights of complete darkness, a harbinger of changes to come. No one knows the true story of how the Tuatha Dé Dannan arrived in Ireland. But everyone knows how they fought their way across the land until it was theirs.

4   When Carman heard about this recent unrest, she saw an opportunity. Perhaps Carman and her power-hungry **progeny** could **usurp** the new leaders if they moved quickly. Barely rested from their last battle, they boarded a boat and sailed toward their next conquest.

5   Carman and her sons came upon the southern shore of Ireland in their mighty vessel. Her heart danced with joy when she saw the green land that lay before them. Countless cattle and crops covered the countryside. She decided that her clan could be content living on that coast. "Soon," she cooed to the terrible trio, "all you see will be ours." The Black-Hearted, the Evil, and the Violent raised their swords, preparing to take the land by force. But wise and noble Carman knew a better way to achieve their aim. She called upon her ancient powers and cast a spell across the land. Her magic turned green to gray as the crops withered away at her words. The soil under the shriveled roots would live to grow plants again, but the Irish would be too weak with hunger to fight. They would need Carman to reverse the spell, so they would welcome her as their queen.

6   But Carman would not succeed. The bellicose brothers did not obey their orders. As Carman slept, they laid siege to the nearest village. Their actions drew the attention of the Tuatha Dé Dannan. Before morning, the brothers had been captured and given the choice of death or exile. They deserted Carman to save themselves. As punishment for her sons' crimes, fair Carman was sealed in a tomb and buried alive. Her sons' **treason** burned in her chest like the fire of a thousand flames. Her cry of grief echoed across the cliffs as breath left her body for the last time. Carman's anguish revealed her remorse and reversed her spell. The farms became more bountiful than ever before, and the Irish were satisfied by the sorceress's sacrifice.

7   Too late, the Irish realized that courageous Carman was not as **callous** as her sons. Deeply affected by her **deplorable** death and her final act of mercy, many mourners held a festival in her honor. The land where her brave bones are buried was renamed Carman to pay tribute to this noble woman's memory.

USING LANGUAGE   CA-CCSS: ELD.PI.11-12.6.c.Ex

Read each sentence. Use a print or online college-level dictionary to look up the precise meaning of each boldfaced word. Then choose the correct meaning.

1. **Hearken!** Attend the tale of noble Carman, the fair.

    ○ Listen!
    ○ Come here!

2. Her three sons, a rank of **rapacious** offspring, were with her always.

    ○ violent
    ○ greedy

3. It is believed that these supernatural beings brought with them three days and three nights of complete darkness, a **harbinger** of changes to come.

    ○ something that comes before something else
    ○ something that causes something else

4. The **bellicose** brothers did not obey their orders.

    ○ likely to fight
    ○ likely to disobey

MEANINGFUL INTERACTIONS   CA-CCSS: ELD.PI.11-12.1.Ex, ELD.PI.11-12.8.Ex

Use the speaking frames to work with a partner or small group to discuss the author's word choice and its effect on readers. Remember that "alliteration" is repeating the same letter sounds at the beginning of more than one word. Then use the self-assessment rubric to evaluate your participation in the discussion.

- In the first paragraph, the narrator speaks directly to readers. This choice is/is not effective because . . .

- One example of alliteration is . . . This phrase has a . . . effect because . . .

- One especially powerful descriptive word or phrase is . . . This word or phrase had a strong effect on me because . . .

- I agree that . . . was a powerful word or phrase, but I think . . . was more powerful because . . .

- One descriptive word or phrase that could be improved is . . .

- I disagree. I think that word or phrase was effective because . . .

SELF-ASSESSMENT RUBRIC   CA-CCSS: ELD.PI.11-12.8.Ex

	4 I did this well.	3 I did this pretty well.	2 I did this a little bit.	1 I did not do this.
I contributed effectively to the group's discussion.				
I evaluated the author's word choice.				
I helped others understand how the author's word choice affected me.				
I provided coherent and well-articulated comments.				

REREAD

Reread paragraphs 1–4 of "The Legend of Carman." After you reread, complete the Using Language and Meaningful Interactions activities.

USING LANGUAGE CA-CCSS: ELD.PII.11-12.3.Ex

Complete the sentences by filling in the blanks.

1. Fill in the blank with a verb in the present tense.

    The storyteller _____ everyone to be quiet and listen to the story.

2. Fill in the blank with a verb in the past tense.

    Carman and her sons _____ from Athens.

3. Fill in the blank with a verb in the progressive aspect.

    Dub, Dother, and Dian _____ with their mother.

4. Fill in the blank with a verb in the perfect aspect.

    The Tuatha Dé Dannan _____ Ireland when Carman decided to go there.

5. Fill in the blank with a verb in the future tense.

    Carman and her sons _____ the Tuatha Dé Dannan.

MEANINGFUL INTERACTIONS CA-CCSS: ELD.PI.11-12.1.Ex, ELD.PI.11-12.6.a.Ex

Based on what you have read in "The Legend of Carman," what do you think about Carman, her sons, and the Tuatha Dé Dannan? Are they heroes or villains? What details support your inferences? Work in small groups to practice sharing your opinions and affirming others, using the speaking frames. Then use the self-assessment rubric to evaluate your participation in the discussion.

- I think Carman is . . . because . . .

- I think Carman's sons are . . . because . . .

- I think the Tuatha Dé Dannan are . . . because . . .

- I think you said that . . .

- Another detail that supports your idea is . . .

- I agree that . . . , but I also think that . . .

 SELF-ASSESSMENT RUBRIC CA-CCSS: ELD.PI.11-12.1.Ex

	4 I did this well.	3 I did this pretty well.	2 I did this a little bit.	1 I did not do this.
I expressed my opinion clearly.				
I listened carefully to others' opinions.				
I affirmed others' opinions.				
I used textual evidence to support my ideas.				

REREAD

Reread paragraphs 5–7 of "The Legend of Carman." After you reread, complete the Using Language and Meaningful Interactions activities.

⚙ USING LANGUAGE   CA-CCSS: ELD.PI.11-12.12.b.Em

Read each sentence. Use your knowledge of suffixes to choose the correct word to fill in the blank.

1. I would _____ help you do the dishes.
   ○ happiness   ○ happily

2. Carlos _____ his birthday last week.
   ○ celebrated   ○ celebration

3. Petra felt a deep _____ when her cat ran away.
   ○ sadly   ○ sadness

4. The bakery burned down in a _____ accident.
   ○ tragedy   ○ tragic

5. The cheerleaders offered _____ when the team was losing.
   ○ encouragement   ○ encouraging

6. The puppy was very _____ after its nap.
   ○ energetic   ○ energy

👥 MEANINGFUL INTERACTIONS   CA-CCSS: ELD.PI.11-12.1.Ex, ELD.PI.11-12.8.Ex

What about the ending of "The Legend of Carman" was most surprising? Why? What evidence from the text supports your opinion? In a whole-class discussion, practice choosing your words carefully to express opinions and evaluating other speakers' word choices. Use the speaking frames to plan your responses and help you with the discussion. You may also want to record the turn-taking rules in the space provided.

- I think . . . was the most surprising part because . . .

- I like what you said about . . . because . . .

- Your point about . . . makes me reconsider my ideas about . . .

Turn-Taking Rules:

- _____

- _____

- _____

- _____

SEARCHING FOR ROBIN HOOD

English Language Development

NON-FICTION

INTRODUCTION

The legend of Robin Hood has been popular for centuries. This article explores the history of the character and the challenges for historians who hope to find the man behind the myth.

"Is any of that true, or is Robin Hood only a myth?"

FIRST READ

1   Let's start with the story, though you may know it already. The year is 1193, and the king of England, Richard the Lionheart, has gone off to fight in the Crusades. Richard's brother, John, has taken over England. A disgraced nobleman named Robin Hood is loyal to Richard. He dislikes John's high taxes. Robin moves to Sherwood Forest and starts a gang of cheerful bandits called the Merry Men. They steal from the rich and give to the poor. Robin, along with Little John, Friar Tuck, and Will Scarlet, terrorize the corrupt sheriff of Nottingham, who can never seem to catch them. In his spare time, Robin romances Maid Marian.

2   Is any of that true, or is Robin Hood only a myth? Many people would like to believe that he really existed. However, the evidence is slim.

3   Robin Hood has been a character in British literature for hundreds of years. The modern conception of Robin Hood dates from the 16th century. In John Major's "History of Greater Britain," written in 1521, Robin Hood is the honorable fallen lord who steals from the rich to give to the poor. Major was the first to include the detail that Robin is the loyal follower of King Richard. This detail is essential because it gives Robin principles. He is a good guy because he only breaks a bad king's laws. When the rightful king returns, Robin stops his **poaching** and thieving ways. He is both a criminal and a patriot.

4   The Robin Hood of the 15th century was quite different. The early Robin Hood was more violent. He hunted the king's deer, yes, but he also murdered feudal lords and sheriffs. This Robin Hood was not a lord but a yeoman, or a common farmer. And his buddies? It turns out that the phrase *merry men,* as in Robin Hood's gang, did not mean *cheerful guys* . . . It meant outlaws.

5   To understand the 15th-century Robin Hood, it's important to know what England was like back then. In the 14th and 15th centuries, the forests of England seemed like wild spaces, but they were reserved exclusively for the

king and his court to hunt in and enjoy. Anyone caught using or hunting in the forests without permission was severely punished. These forest laws were incredibly unpopular. It's no surprise that **ballad** writers created a folk hero who **flaunted** them. Audiences loved the stories of a commoner fighting against the powerful rulers.

6   Why, then, was Robin Hood promoted to **philanthropic** nobleman in later years? It may have been the changing interests of the audience. In the 16th century, the distribution of wealth and land was still deeply unfair, but the violence of the earlier medieval era had passed.

7   Still, the character is even older than the 15th century **anti-establishment** outlaw. The oldest mention of Robin Hood appears in William Langland's poem *Piers Plowman,* written in 1377. It's simply an allusion to "rymes of Robyn Hood." This shows that ballads about Robin Hood were already a part of popular culture.

8   A historian would have to go back further than 1377 to find the man behind the myth. But that historian would have a big problem. As early as the 13th century, record keepers and courts used the terms Robehod, Rabunhod, or Robynhod as a general name for outlaws. It was a medieval "Benedict Arnold" or "Scrooge"—a proper name used as a label for a certain type of person. Historians can find a man called William Robehod, a fugitive named in court records in 1261, but more research shows that William's surname was le Fevere. Robehod was a label applied by a clerk. Furthermore, William "Robehod" le Fevere's actions are long forgotten. He may have been an outlaw, but that doesn't make him *the* Robin Hood.

9   If Robin Hood was used as another word for *outlaw* in 1261, then logically the character goes back even further. Unfortunately, the trail goes cold. Looking for a single outlaw who inspired these stories that long ago is impossible. Besides, the myth has grown bigger than the deeds of a single man. If any record of a real Robin Hood were to surface, we'd likely be disappointed.

USING LANGUAGE   CA-CCSS: ELD.PI.11-12.6.c.Ex

Read each word. Complete the chart by choosing the meaning of the affix from the options. Some options may be used more than once. Then write the meaning of the word into the fourth column.

Affix Meaning Options			
not	opposite of	having a certain quality	full of

Word	Affix	Affix Meaning	Word Meaning
dislikes	dis-		
honorable	-able		
cheerful	-ful		
unpopular	un-		
impossible	im-		

MEANINGFUL INTERACTIONS CA-CCSS: ELD.PI.11-12.10.b.Ex

Work with your partner or group to summarize the key ideas in "Searching for Robin Hood," using the writing frames below. Then use the self-assessment rubric to evaluate your participation in the activity.

First, the author _____.

He says that Robin Hood is _____.

In paragraph 3, the author states that _____.

Before the 16th century, Robin Hood was _____.

This change may have happened because _____.

Writers of ballads used the Robin Hood character to _____.

To find the real man behind Robin Hood stories, a historian would have to _____
_____.

The problem with looking at old records is _____.

SELF-ASSESSMENT RUBRIC CA-CCSS: ELD.PI.11-12.10.b.Ex

	4 I did this well.	3 I did this pretty well.	2 I did this a little bit.	1 I did not do this.
I took an active part with others in doing the activity.				
I contributed effectively to the group's decisions.				
I identified the key ideas in the text.				
I helped others understand the key ideas in the text.				
I completed the writing frames carefully and accurately.				

REREAD

Reread paragraphs 1–5 of "Searching for Robin Hood." After you reread, complete the Using Language and Meaningful Interactions activities.

USING LANGUAGE CA-CCSS: ELD.PI.11-12.6.c.Ex

Read the word from the text. Complete the chart by selecting other words from the options below that have similar meanings but weaker or stronger connotations. Use a dictionary or thesaurus if needed.

Connotation Options							
radiant	virtuous	nice	very	average	enormously	happy	low

Weaker Connotation	Word from Text	Stronger Connotation
	cheerful	
	incredibly	
	common	
	honorable	

MEANINGFUL INTERACTIONS CA-CCSS: ELD.PI.11-12.7.Ex

Review the word choices from the Using Language activity. With your group, use the speaking frames to discuss what effect the author created with those words. Then, evaluate how successfully the author uses language throughout the passage. Finally, use the self-assessment rubric to evaluate your participation in the discussion.

- The word . . . creates a . . . effect.

- Why do you think the author chose the word . . . ?

- This word fits in with this passage because . . .

- The author was successful / not successful in using language throughout the passage because . . .

- Which word would be more effective than . . . ?

- What other words does the author use to create an effect?

 SELF-ASSESSMENT RUBRIC CA-CCSS: ELD.PI.11-12.1.Ex

	4 I did this well.	3 I did this pretty well.	2 I did this a little bit.	1 I did not do this.
I explained the author's word choices clearly.				
I evaluated the effect created by the author.				
I asked and answered relevant questions to keep the discussion moving.				
I was courteous when persuading others to share my view.				

REREAD

Reread paragraphs 6–9 of "Searching for Robin Hood." After you reread, complete the Using Language and Meaningful Interactions activities.

⚙ USING LANGUAGE   CA-CCSS: ELD.PII.11-12.3.Ex

Complete the sentences by filling in the blanks.

1. Fill in the blank with a verb in the past tense.

    The author of the poem *Piers Plowman* _____ the "rymes of Robyn Hood."

2. Fill in the blank with a verb in the simple past tense.

    People in the 14th century _____ ballads about Robin Hood.

3. Fill in the blank with a verb in the past progressive tense.

    Clerks _____ the terms "Robehod," "Rabunhod," and "Robynhod" for outlaws in general.

4. Fill in the blank with a verb in the past tense.

    The name William Robehod _____ in court records in 1261.

5. Fill in the blank with a verb in the past perfect tense.

    Historical records _____ that there is likely no real person behind the myth of Robin Hood.

👥 MEANINGFUL INTERACTIONS   CA-CCSS: ELD.PI.11-12.1.Ex

Do you think Robin Hood really existed? Why or why not? Draw a conclusion based on the information in "Searching for Robin Hood." Use the speaking frames to participate in the whole-class discussion.

- I think Robin Hood did/did not really exist because . . .

- Evidence from the text that supports my conclusion is . . .

- . . . , it's your turn. What conclusion did you draw from the text?

- What you said is interesting. Have you thought about . . . ?

EXTENDED WRITING PROJECT

WRITE

Extended Writing Project Prompt and Directions:

Think about the heroes in the selections you have read... how does a legendary hero help shape the history of a... hero (or heroine) modeled on the style of *Le Morte d'A...* a real, heroic person you know, or you can write about... your narrative in a real or imagined world.

Your narrative should include:

- an engaging opening that introduces the characters and setting
- vivid descriptions of the setting and characters
- a logically organized sequence of events
- an ending that effectively wraps up the story
- an underlying theme or message

NOTES

EXTENDED WRITING PROJECT
NARRATIVE WRITING

NARRATIVE WRITING

WRITING PROMPT

Think about the heroes in the selections you have read. What qualities define a hero, and how does a legendary hero help shape the history of a nation? Write a narrative about a hero (or heroine) modeled on the style of *Le Morte d'Arthur* or *Beowulf*. You can write about a real, heroic person you know, or you can write about a fictional character. You can set your narrative in a real or imagined world.

Your narrative should include:

- an engaging opening that introduces the characters and setting
- vivid descriptions of the setting and characters
- a logically organized sequence of events
- an ending that effectively wraps up the story
- an underlying theme or message

Narrative writing tells a story of real or imagined experiences or events. Narratives can be fiction or nonfiction. Fictional narratives can take the form of novels, short stories, poems, or plays. Nonfiction narratives are true stories, often expressed in memoirs or diary entries, personal essays or letters, autobiographies or biographies, or histories. Many narratives have a clearly identified narrator who tells the story as it unfolds. In nonfiction narratives, the author usually tells the story. In fictional narratives, the narrator can be a character in the story or someone outside of the story. Effective narrative writing uses storytelling techniques, relevant descriptive details, and well-structured event sequences to convey a story to readers. The features of narrative writing include:

- setting
- characters

- plot
- conflict
- theme
- point of view

As you actively participate in this extended writing project, you will receive more instructions and practice to help you craft each of the elements of narrative writing.

 ## STUDENT MODEL

Before you get started on your own narrative, begin by reading this narrative that one student wrote in response to the writing prompt. As you read this student model, highlight and annotate the features of narrative writing that the student included in her story.

Lady Letha, Knight of Mordred

It is a day of destiny. My lord Mordred's army is to meet with the forces of the unspeakable tyrant, Arthur. I feel strong, and my brothers-in-arms are showing great courage as they prepare to face the enemy this morning. We are to meet on the field at Camlann. It is said that Sir Mordred is to sign a treaty with his father, the villain. But my lord has told us that if any of the enemy draws his sword, we are to attack without mercy.

. . .

There was no easy path for me to become a knight. I was a servant of my lady Morgan Le Fay. At first men laughed when they learned of my intention and told me the only sword I'd ever swing was a bread knife. Yet the knights who were devoted to my lady were not like the other men. Though perhaps at first they thought it amusing to instruct me in the skills of swordplay, as I practiced I became strong and skilled. They grew impressed. When I told my lady of my intentions, she smiled and gave her blessing to my undertaking. More importantly, she supplied me with a sword that she said had special powers only for me. The sword was called Nightshade. She also ordered a suit of armor to be crafted for me by the finest smith in Rheged.

NOTES

During my first battle, Nightshade moved as if it had a mind of its own. Some fierce opponents who sneered at me found themselves without heads. I fought near Sir Mordred to make sure he was safe. When I saw an enemy try to sneak up, I showed no pity. By the end of the battle I had men running from me like mice fleeing a cat.

. . .

As we muster in the field in the morning mist at Camlann, the enemy appears out of the fog like evil ghosts. We drink a toast to each other, and all seems well at first. But suddenly one of Arthur's knights draws a sword, and we quickly fall into battle formation. Bloodcurdling screams arise as the armies charge at each other with great determination.

My brothers and I embrace our leader's command and show our foes no mercy. Yet they too fight with great power, and no side can gain the advantage. I position myself near dear Sir Mordred and watch for any potential threats. While the sun rises, the fog vanishes and the glint of sunlight off the warriors' armor is like the lightning that accompanies the thunder of hundreds of sword-strikes.

The deaths and terrible injuries mount. The shouts of despair rise to a level nearly even to that of the shouts of rage as warriors charge at new opponent after new opponent. My lord calls out encouragement to his noble warriors, but at times I think I can hear him choke back tears as he watches much of his army wilting along with that of the enemy.

As the sun reaches the midpoint of its afternoon descent, several of Arthur's knights begin to make steady progress toward my beloved leader. I rally some of my friends who still have their strength. Sir Mordred's favorite knight, Sir Lewis, nudges me and points at an enemy with his sword. "We must stop Sir Lucan. He is a mighty knight who can do our lord great harm."

We struggle in hand-to-hand combat with those knights till twilight. Though we have been keeping Sir Mordred safe, Sir Lucan is edging closer and closer to him. As I see him deal Sir Lewis an awful clout to the helm, I step forward and swing Nightshade with all my might at a gap in his armor near the hip. I expect to cleave him in two, yet he is able to thrust his dagger at me even as he limps away, badly hurt. His dagger slices my neck, and I cry out.

I feel my life force slipping away. Through the haze of fatigue and pain I see the approach of the enemy king, one of the few men still able to fight. He charges hard at my Lord Mordred, who turns to face his father with grim resolve. With great skill and effort the cursed monarch runs my lord through with a spear, but with the last of his strength my lord lashes out with a mighty blow of his sword at Arthur's head, and I know neither man will live to see the morning.

I die. I die content that I have given my best service to my lord and that the tyranny of Arthur has died with me.

 THINK QUESTIONS

1. What is the setting of this narrative? Refer to two or more details from the text to support your understanding of why this student has included certain details to convey the setting of the story to readers.

2. Describe the conflict of this story. Explain which details this student has chosen to include in this story and why.

3. Write two or three sentences explaining the point of view this student chose for this narrative and the details that reveal the narrator's point of view.

4. Thinking about the writing prompt, which selections, Blasts, or other resources would you like to use to create your own narrative? What are some ideas that you may want to develop into your own narratives?

5. Based on what you have read, listened to, or researched, how would you answer the question *How do legends transform history?* What are some ways in which you might include special qualities in the hero in the narrative you'll be developing?

NOTES

SKILL:
ORGANIZE
NARRATIVE
WRITING

⭐ DEFINE

Every **narrative**, be it a novel or a seven-word story, revolves around a **conflict**, or a problem that the characters must face or overcome. A conflict can be external—a knight fighting a dragon, for example—or internal—such as a teenager struggling with the death of a friend.

To describe the events, a narrative needs a **narrator.** The narrator can be a character in the story, telling the story from the **first-person point of view.** Or the narrator can be outside the story, telling it from **third-person point of view.** If the narrator knows the thoughts and the actions of all of the characters, then that point of view is called **third-person omniscient.** When the narrator knows the thoughts and actions of only one character, then the point of view is called **third-person limited.** Whichever type of narrator you choose, make sure you are consistent throughout the story.

In a narrative, **characters** need to be introduced and developed. If they aren't, your audience will be confused. Details about the characters can be revealed slowly or all at once, but characters typically develop and change over the course of the narrative.

••• IDENTIFICATION AND APPLICATION

- Present the conflict, or problem, early in the story to engage readers and keep them reading.
  - › Explain the conflict's significance to the characters. Why is this conflict worth reading about?
  - › In a hero narrative, the conflict is often related to a quest, or something the hero wants to obtain or accomplish, and the obstacles faced in pursuit of that goal.
- Establish a clear and consistent point of view.
  - › Effective narratives can use first-person, third-person, or third-person omniscient point of view.

› First-person point of view uses first-person pronouns, such as I, me, and my. First-person narrators are limited to a single view of events but also make the narration more personal and emotionally involving. In addition, first-person narrators may or may not be reliable in their narration of events, meaning readers must use details to make inferences.

› Third-person point of view uses third-person pronouns, such as he, they, and hers. An advantage of third-person narrators is their ability to be everywhere the author wants to place them in a story, and they are reliable. On the other hand, third-person narrators are distanced emotionally since they are not personally invested in the outcome of events or in the characters.

• Introduce and develop your characters.

› As a writer, know your characters' motivations. Ask yourself: Why do they act the way they do? Does the reader need more background to understand this character?

› Characters can be introduced all at once or over the course of the narrative.

› In most narratives, the main character should grow or change in some way by the end of the story.

• Create a smooth progression of events.

› Use clear transitions and signal words.

 MODEL

A hero narrative generally involves two important things: first, a hero, who is the main character; and second, a quest, or task to complete. The student model narrative "Lady Letha, Knight of Mordred" presents the **main character** and **narrator** right in the title. Many hero stories and legends are named for their main character, including *Beowulf* and *Le Morte d'Arthur* ("The Death of Arthur," in French).

The **point of view** is established in the opening lines of the narrative. In addition, the hero's quest is made clear.

It is a day of destiny. **My** *lord Mordred's army is* **to meet with the forces of the unspeakable tyrant, Arthur.** *I feel strong, and* **my** *brothers-in-arms are showing great courage as they prepare to face the enemy this morning.*

The narrator uses **first-person** pronouns, including *I* and *my*. That means that the narrator is speaking from first-person point of view and that the narrator is also part of the story. In this case, the narrator is the hero, Lady Letha. Her quest is "to meet with the forces of the unspeakable tyrant, Arthur" and, it is implied, defeat him.

In the first paragraph, the author presents the **conflict**, or problem, of the story: "My lord Mordred's army is to meet with the forces of the unspeakable tyrant, Arthur." This conflict covers the same time period as the selection from *Le Morte d'Arthur*—Arthur's final battle, at Camlann. The details connect this original story to an established legend.

In the next paragraph, the student writer develops the character of Lady Letha. The first sentence alerts the reader to the hero's background.

There was no easy path for me to become a knight. I was a servant of my lady Morgan Le Fay. *At first men laughed when they learned of* **my intention** *and told me the only sword I'd ever swing was a bread knife. Yet the knights who were devoted to my lady were not like the other men. Though perhaps at first they thought it amusing to instruct me in the skills of swordplay, as I practiced* **I became strong and skilled.**

This paragraph is a flashback, because the verb tense changes from present to past: "There was no easy path for me to become a knight." Not only is this character fighting against a beloved hero, King Arthur, but she is a woman who has become a knight. This short sentence adds greatly to our understanding of her character as well as to the story's plot. As readers, we learn Letha's background from her memory: "I was a servant." She dreamed of being a knight, calling it "my intention," but most men did not want to teach her to fight. Eventually, she impressed her teachers and "became strong and skilled." In this short paragraph, the writer shows a reader that Letha is determined, hardworking, and a skilled knight. These character details set up the adventure to come.

PRACTICE

Think about the kind of hero who might be the central character in your narrative. What qualities or character traits might he or she possess, and what techniques might you use to develop this hero? What is the hero's quest? Write a short paragraph that introduces and describes this character from the third-person point of view. Then write another short paragraph that introduces and describes this character from the first-person point of view, where the narrator is a character in the story. Exchange papers with a partner and evaluate each other's work. Which version do you think works best and is the most effective way to introduce the character, his or her quest, and the conflict he or she faces?

PREWRITE

CA-CCSS: CA.W.11-12.3a, CA.W.11-12.4, CA.W.11-12.5, CA.W.11-12.6, CA.W.11-12.9a, CA.SL.11-12.1, CA.L.11-12.1a

WRITING PROMPT

Think about the heroes in the selections you have read. What qualities define a hero, and how does a legendary hero help shape the history of a nation? Write a narrative about a hero (or heroine) modeled on the style of *Le Morte d'Arthur* or *Beowulf*. You can write about a real, heroic person you know, or you can write about a fictional character. You can set your narrative in a real or imagined world.

Your narrative should include:

- an engaging opening that introduces the characters and setting
- vivid descriptions of the setting and characters
- a logically organized sequence of events
- an ending that effectively wraps up the story
- an underlying theme or message

In addition to studying an author's approach to audience and purpose before writing a narrative, as well as how an author begins organizing a story, you have been reading and learning about stories that feature heroes. In the extended writing project, you will use those narratives as models to compose your own hero narrative.

Since the topic of your narrative will be a hero story, you'll want to think about how heroes were developed in the selections you've read. Consider the elements of narrative writing that the author of the student model narrative and *Le Morte d'Arthur* included in her narrative. What makes the main character a hero? What problem or conflict does each author create? How does the story's point of view enhance the narrative?

Make a list of the answers to these questions for the model or *Le Morte d'Arthur* and your own hero. As you write down your ideas, look for patterns that begin to emerge. How are your hero's characteristics similar to or different from Arthur's or Letha's? How do heroes in these stories react to conflict? Looking for these patterns may help you solidify the ideas you want to explore in your narrative. Follow this model to help you get started with your own prewriting:

Hero: Lady Letha, a knight of Mordred who is fighting against King Arthur

Characters: Letha, Morgan le Fay, Mordred, Sir Lewis

Setting: battlefield of Camlann

Conflict: Letha fights in the final battle of Arthur and Mordred, on the side of Mordred

Plot: Lady Letha, a knight, is on the battlefield. She flashes back to her training as a knight and the hardships she faced. Then the story returns to the battle. Letha is killed protecting Mordred, who also dies along with King Arthur.

Point of View: first person, from Letha's perspective; she believes her deeds are heroic

Theme: Female knights can be as capable as male ones, but good still conquers evil.

SKILL:
NARRATIVE
SEQUENCING

 DEFINE

A writer carefully crafts the **sequence of events** in a narrative – **exposition, rising action, climax, falling action,** and **resolution.** The events in a story build toward a specific **outcome** – whether that's a full resolution of the story's conflict, the main character's growth over the course of the story, or a pervading sense of foreboding, danger, or suspense.

The sequence of events also has to make sense. The writer has to provide details – or else deliberately leave them out – to make the story thought-provoking and entertaining. To effectively build to the outcome of the narrative, the writer also carefully crafts his or her language to achieve the perfect **tone** – suspense, humor, hatred, or contentment are examples of tones.

The author thinks about his or her audience and the purpose for writing when he or she is deciding which events to include in the story, and what tone to use. For instance, a mystery writer will sequence events leading toward the resolution of the mystery and will use words that help create that sense of suspense.

 IDENTIFICATION AND APPLICATION

- A narrative outline, especially in the form of a plot diagram, can help writers organize a sequence of events before they begin writing a story.
  - › A narrative outline may follow this framework: exposition, rising action (conflict), climax, falling action, resolution.
  - › For a hero narrative, a standard narrative outline is useful. However, not all narratives follow this standard progression. Some narratives, such as "slice of life" stories, focus on character rather than on plot.
- The exposition contains essential information for the reader, such as characters, setting, and the problem or conflict the characters will face.

- In the rising action, a writer begins to develop plot and character.
  - › The rising action begins with what is sometimes called a trigger, or an inciting incident. The trigger is the event that sets all the other events of the plot in motion.
  - › The incident that triggers plot events to come may be contained in a line of dialogue, a chance encounter between characters, the arrival of a character, a deliberate statement made by the author, or in any number of other ways depending on the type of story being told.
- The climax is the turning point in the story, often where the most exciting action takes place. At the climax, the protagonist often acts on a decision or faces the conflict.
- The details and events that follow the climax make up the falling action. These events are often the results of choices made by the protagonist during the climax.
- The story generally ends in a resolution of the conflict. Depending on their purpose, some authors make deliberate choices to leave plot points unresolved, or open-ended.
- The story's tone is achieved by careful word choice as well as the events of the narrative.
  - › Use a thesaurus to replace general words ("sad") with specific, vivid synonyms ("despondent").
  - › Describe events in ways that reveal character traits and help lead to the story's outcome.
- An author's audience and purpose dictate the sequence of events as well as the tone the author uses.

 MODEL

The author of the student model narrative "Lady Letha, Knight of Mordred" used a story plot diagram to outline and organize his ideas. This student's story was based on *Le Morte d'Arthur*. Look at the outline and think about how you will outline and organize the sequence of events in your story.

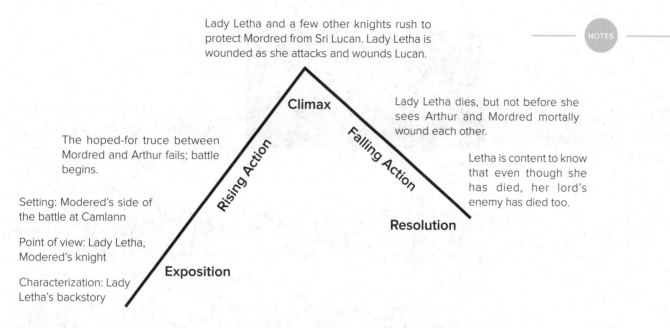

Lady Letha and a few other knights rush to protect Mordred from Sri Lucan. Lady Letha is wounded as she attacks and wounds Lucan.

Climax

Lady Letha dies, but not before she sees Arthur and Mordred mortally wound each other.

Rising Action

Falling Action

The hoped-for truce between Mordred and Arthur fails; battle begins.

Letha is content to know that even though she has died, her lord's enemy has died too.

Setting: Modered's side of the battle at Camlann

Resolution

Point of view: Lady Letha, Modered's knight

Exposition

Characterization: Lady Letha's backstory

The author of the student model chose to intersperse key events that are not always in sequence. Reread these sentences that span paragraphs 1 and 2:

....But my lord has told us that if any of the enemy draws his sword, we are to attack without mercy.

. . .

There was no easy path for me to become a knight. I was a servant of my lady Morgan Le Fay.

The author has interrupted her narrative's linear sequence to provide **exposition**, in this case a backstory about the narrator. This method of sequencing also helps to generate a specific tone, in this case a feeling of **suspense**. The first section before the break ends with "we are to attack without mercy," quickly followed by, "There was no easy path for me to become a knight." Readers know they will have to wait for the battle scene, which they can infer will follow this background section.

 PRACTICE

To organize and sequence your hero narrative, complete a story structure map with information as on the diagram that follows the Model. When you are finished, trade with a partner and offer each other feedback. Is there a clear narrative sequence that introduces characters, the conflict, and events that follow? Does your partner offer enough exposition? How does the rising action lead to the climax? Do the falling action and resolution follow logically from what came before? Does the sequence build toward a particular outcome? Offer each other suggestions, and remember that they are most helpful when they are constructive.

NOTES

PLAN

CA-CCSS: CA.W.11-12.3a, CA.W.11-12.3c, CA.W.11-12.5, CA.W.11-12.6, CA.W.11-12.10, CA.SL.11-12.1a, CA.SL.11-12.1b, CA.SL.11-12.1c, CA.SL.11-12.1d

WRITING PROMPT

Think about the heroes in the selections you have read. What qualities define a hero, and how does a legendary hero help shape the history of a nation? Write a narrative about a hero (or heroine) modeled on the style of *Le Morte d'Arthur* or *Beowulf*. You can write about a real, heroic person you know, or you can write about a fictional character. You can set your narrative in a real or imagined world.

Your narrative should include:

- an engaging opening that introduces the characters and setting
- vivid descriptions of the setting and characters
- a logically organized sequence of events
- an ending that effectively wraps up the story
- an underlying theme or message

Use the information you included in your Story Structure Map to write a one-paragraph summary that tells what will happen in your narrative. Do not worry about including all of the details now. Your summary should focus on developing the sequence of events for your narrative. Note places where the features of narrative writing would be most effective. You will use this short summary as a jumping off point when you write a full draft of your narrative.

Consider the following questions as you write your summary:

- Are there ideas in your Story Structure Map that you might wish to change or adjust? How will those adjustments affect your narrative's outcome?
- What details and events are most important in the rising action of the narrative?

- What is the purpose of the narrative's climax?
- How will you lead readers toward a resolution of the narrative? How will the protagonist hero change or grow?
- Is there anything you want to withhold from the reader? What purpose would that serve?
- What do you hope readers will take away from your hero narrative?

Please note that excerpts and passages in the StudySync® library and this workbook are intended as touchstones to generate interest in an author's work. The excerpts and passages do not substitute for the reading of entire texts, and StudySync® strongly recommends that students seek out and purchase the whole literary or informational work in order to experience it as the author intended. Links to online resellers are available in our digital library. In addition, complete works may be ordered through an authorized reseller by filling out and returning to StudySync® the order form enclosed in this workbook.

Reading & Writing Companion   **101**

NOTES

SKILL:
INTRODUCTIONS

 DEFINE

The **introduction** is the opening to a story. An introduction needs to grab readers' attention and entice them to keep reading. In a short narrative, an introduction may introduce the problem, or conflict, as well as the main characters and other essential details that readers will need in order to follow the story.

Narratives can be introduced in any number of ways. Some introductions reveal hints of an internal conflict, as these famous opening lines from the novel *Anna Karenina* do: "All happy families are alike; each unhappy family is unhappy in its own way." Other introductions may use sensory language to throw readers right into the thick of an external conflict, as with these lines from "An Occurrence at Owl Creek Bridge" by Ambrose Bierce:

> A man stood upon a railroad bridge in northern Alabama, looking down into the swift water twenty feet below. The man's hands were behind his back, the wrists bound with a cord. A rope closely encircled his neck. It was attached to a stout cross-timber above his head and the slack fell to the level of his knees. Some loose boards laid upon the ties supporting the rails of the railway supplied a footing for him and his executioners - two private soldiers of the Federal army, directed by a sergeant who in civil life may have been a deputy sheriff.

An introduction can present something unexpected to the reader, who will then want to read more, as in this opening line from George Orwell's futuristic novel, *1984*: "It was a bright cold day in April, and the clocks were striking thirteen."

However a writer chooses to introduce a short narrative, the details should transport the reader into the world of the story.

IDENTIFICATION AND APPLICATION

- The introduction and conclusion frame the events of a narrative.
- The introduction is the author's way of inviting readers into a story. A strong opening line or some other narrative "hook," such as an exciting moment, a surprising moment, or a thoughtful comment made by the narrator or main character can help to hook the reader.
- The introduction usually provides exposition about characters, setting, and conflict.
- Use the introduction to orient the reader in the fictional world you are creating in your narrative. Make sure that you are able to answer the following questions with your introduction:
  › Who are the characters?
  › What is the setting?
  › What is the conflict?
- Include sensory details (e.g., sights, sounds, smells, tastes, etc.) to capture a reader's attention and draw them into the narrative.

 ## MODEL

The author of the student model narrative "Lady Letha, Knight of Mordred" begins the narrative *in media res* - in the middle of the action. Notice how the details pull the reader right into the action of the hero story:

> **It is a day of destiny. My lord Mordred's army is to meet with the forces of the unspeakable tyrant, Arthur.** I feel strong, and my brothers-in-arms are showing great courage as they prepare to face the enemy this morning. **We are to meet on the field at Camlann.** It is said that Sir Mordred is to sign a treaty with his father, **the villain.** But my lord has told us that if any of the enemy draws his sword, we are to attack without mercy.

The writer uses the first sentence, "It is a day of destiny," to grab the reader's attention. The readers are left wondering why this day is so important. In the second sentence, the writer introduces the conflict, or problem: "My lord Mordred's army is to meet with the forces of the unspeakable tyrant, Arthur." The **introduction** goes on to provide the setting, the "field at Camlann." In a tight paragraph, the author has provided context (the King Arthur legend), the conflict to be decided (a battle between Mordred and Arthur), the hero (Lady Letha), her quest and the stakes (to defeat Arthur for Sir Mordred), and the war-like tone ("attack without mercy").

NOTES

The narrator describes King Arthur, the popular hero, as "the unspeakable tyrant" and "the villain." This provides clues to the reader of the perspective of the narrator and creates interest in the character. While the introduction provides a lot of the basic *who, what, where* answers, it also leaves enough mystery to engage the reader in the story.

⚡ PRACTICE

Write an introduction for your narrative essay that invites the reader into the story. You may want to introduce the main characters, setting, or conflict. When you are finished, trade with a partner and offer each other feedback. Did your partner create an interesting world with interesting characters? Were you engaged? Did you want to keep reading and learn more? Offer each other suggestions, and remember that they are most helpful when they are constructive.

SKILL:
NARRATIVE
TECHNIQUES

 DEFINE

To write a story, authors use a variety of techniques to develop the plot and characters. Narrative techniques include dialogue, description, pacing, reflection, and multiple plot lines.

Most narratives have **dialogue,** or the conversation between two or more characters. Dialogue can be used to develop characters or to move the plot forward. Writers use **description** outside of dialogue to describe the setting, characters, and events. Strong description often includes figurative language.

Pacing is the speed at which a story is told. A writer can play with pacing. For example, a writer might speed up the pace as the story nears a climax, or slow down the pace to reflect a character's indecision.

During a story, the author or narrator might want to comment on the action. This technique is called **reflection.** Reflection is effective in a personal narrative, especially in the introduction or conclusion.

While most stories have one plot, some have **multiple plot lines.** To create multiple plot lines, a narrator might spend one chapter or section following one character and then jump to another character who is doing a separate, but related, task.

 IDENTIFICATION AND APPLICATION

- Rather than relying only on a narrator to tell the reader what has happened, use dialogue to allow the characters to do the explaining.
  › Set all dialogue off in quotation marks and clearly note who is speaking.
  › Use vocabulary, punctuation, and sentence lengths in the dialogue that reflect the way a given character would speak.

NOTES

- Use vivid description to engage readers and help them visualize the characters, setting, and other elements in the narrative.
  - › Only include descriptions relevant to the reader's understanding of the element being described.
  - › Consider how descriptions contribute to the reader's involvement in the action, feelings toward characters, and understanding of the story's theme.
- Use pacing effectively to convey a sense of urgency or calm in a narrative. A writer controls pacing with, for example, sentence lengths, incorporation of dialogue, descriptive details, punctuation, and through the release of information that furthers or suspends the action.
- Consider using reflection to show the reader how the narrator or other characters feel about the events. Reflection can be used with first-person narrators who are in the middle of the action as well as with third-person narrators who comment on the action.
- Multiple plot lines can be an effective way to show how multiple characters interact when they aren't together.
  - › When using multiple plot lines, clearly convey to readers which plot line they're reading at that moment. Use character names, setting details, and details about specific events to alert readers to each plot line.
  - › Keep transitions clear. The use of a section break or a change in chapters can indicate a change to a new plot line.
  - › Think about how all the plot lines will intersect by the story's end.
- Use any combination of the above narrative techniques to develop experiences, events, and/or characters.

 MODEL

The author of *Le Morte d'Arthur* uses a combination of **narrative techniques** to develop the events leading up to Arthur's death. These techniques include dialogue, description, and pacing.

The novel is narrated in the third person, but rather than use the narrator to tell the reader everything that happens, the author uses **dialogue** to move the plot forward. Look at this exchange, introduced by the narrator:

> Then they heard people cry out in the field.
> **"Now go thou, Sir Lucan,"** said the king, **"and let me know what that noise in the field betokens."**
> So Sir Lucan departed slowly, for he was grievously wounded in many places;...

NOTES

Suppose the author had written this instead of the dialogue: *Arthur was concerned about the people in the field, so he sent Sir Lucan out to check on them*. While such a sentence conveys the king's request, the opportunity to reveal character is lost. Instead of a brief narration, the author uses a line of dialogue that allows the king to show his politeness, "Now go thou, Sir Lucan," as well as his kingly poise given the situation: "let me know what that noise in the field betokens". By showing the king's character through the dialogue, the author involves the reader emotionally in the fates of King Arthur, Sir Lucan, and the other knights.

The author uses effective **description** of the activities in the field, the details conveyed through the third-person narrator:

> So **Sir Lucan departed slowly, for he was grievously wounded in many places;** as he went **he saw and noticed by the moonlight** how **plunderers and robbers** had come into the field **to plunder and to rob** many a full noble knight of **brooches and beads,** of many a good ring, and of many a rich jewel. And **whoever was not fully dead, the robbers slew them f**or their armor and their riches.

The narrator explains why Sir Lucan moved so slowly, "for he was grievously wounded in many places", and develops Sir Lucan's findings through restatement. Phrases such as "saw and noticed," "plunderers and robbers," and "to plunder and to rob" reinforce the events but also heighten the horrible acts and their aftermath. The use of alliteration in "brooches and beads" helps to emphasize that the knights lost their lives for mere jewelry. The reader can easily picture what is happening in the field that is causing a commotion.

Not all scenes or events need to be lingered over and visualized so completely as that scene. Sometimes, to increase the **pace,** the author describes a conversation quickly:

> When Sir Lucan understood this work, he came back to the king as quickly as he could **and told him all that he had heard and seen.**
> "Therefore, by my counsel," said Sir Lucan, "it is best that we bring you to some town."

In this example, the author is able to jump over the conversation to keep the plot moving along since there is no need for readers to hear details they have already read be repeated fully through dialogue. The actual words that Sir Lucan uses to describe the events in the field are not important, only his conclusion that King Arthur is not safe in the chapel.

NOTES

 PRACTICE

Write a short scene that conveys a point of rising action in your narrative and that includes either dialogue or a scene of personal reflection. As you plan to write your scene, think about the setting, the characters, and the conflict they face in your story. Use the narrative techniques introduced in the lesson, such as dialogue, description, and pacing, to guide readers through your paragraph. When you are finished, trade scenes with a partner and offer one another feedback. Did your partner create a believable conversation or an effective moment of reflection? Were you interested and engaged in the scene? Did you want to continue reading to find out what happened next? Offer each other suggestions, and keep in mind that feedback is most helpful when it is offered in a constructive and respectful manner.

SKILL:
CONCLUSIONS

 DEFINE

The **conclusion** is the end of a narrative. The conclusion is the reader's final experience with a narrative. It should include the resolution of the conflict that propelled the events of the story and provide readers with a sense of closure. A strong conclusion follows logically from what the characters have experienced over the course of the narrative, coming out of the climax and the events in the falling action. Sometimes the story's ending may be somewhat open-ended, but if readers are left guessing or wondering, they should still feel that the conclusion connects with the events that have come before. Whatever the style of conclusion, the ending of events should incorporate the author's message, or theme.

 IDENTIFICATION AND APPLICATION

- Along with the introduction, a conclusion frames the events of a narrative.
- The conclusion is the author's farewell to the reader, after the reader has experienced the events of the story.
- The conclusion must provide the resolution of the conflict (how the problem is solved).
  › The conclusion may reflect on the events in the story.
  › In a hero narrative, a hero's quest should be fulfilled, or explained if not fulfilled.
- Writers may include descriptive details to arouse an emotional response in a reader as the story ends.

 MODEL

Having introduced the student model narrative "Lady Letha, Knight of Mordred" with the title character's determination to help Mordred defeat King

Arthur in battle, the author ends the story with an appropriately dramatic conclusion:

> **I feel my life-force slipping away. Through the haze of fatigue and pain I see the approach of the enemy king, one of the few men still able to fight.** He charges hard at my Lord Mordred, who turns to face his father with grim resolve. With great skill and effort the cursed monarch runs my lord through with a spear, but with the last of his strength my lord lashes out with a mighty blow of his sword at Arthur's head, and **I know neither man will live to see the morning.**
>
> I die. **I die content that I have given my best service to my lord and that the tyranny of Arthur has died with me.**

The conclusion follows logically from the events that have come before, for since the narrative's beginning a battle has been promised to the reader. Letha describes events to the last, beginning, "I feel my life-force slipping away." The dramatic use of the phrase "life-force" is in keeping with Letha's character. To demonstrate her will to see the battle through, she says, "Through the haze of fatigue and pain I see the approach of the enemy king, one of the few men still able to fight." The author includes descriptive details, such as "haze of fatigue" and "one of the few men still able to fight," that give readers a sense of the experience of a final battle.

Epics and legends often conclude with the death of the hero - including Arthur (in this unit's excerpt from *Le Morte d'Arthur*) and Beowulf (at the end of the complete poem). These heroes often succumb to death while sacrificing themselves for others. Lady Letha follows this pattern, dying to protect her lord, Sir Mordred. She says of Arthur and Mordred, "...I know neither man will live to see the morning." Her role as narrator continues as she reveals that despite her efforts, Mordred dies too - though she is consoled with the knowledge that Arthur perished as well because of her heroic efforts. The author concludes with Letha's narration, "...the tyranny of Arthur has died with me." However, readers may sense irony in this, for it is Arthur's legend that will live on, and not Letha's service to Mordred.

 PRACTICE

Write a conclusion for your hero narrative. First, use your Story Structure Map and summary to list the characters and major events leading up the end of your narrative. Follow this list with a draft of your concluding paragraph or paragraphs. When you are finished, trade with a partner and offer each other feedback. Based on the listed events and characters, how effectively did the writer wrap up the story? What final thought did the writer leave you with? Offer each other suggestions, and remember that they are most helpful when they are constructive.

DRAFT

CA-CCSS: CA.W.11-12.3a, CA.W.11-12.3e, CA.W.11-12.4, CA.W.11-12.5, CA.W.11-12.6, CA.W.11-12.9a, CA.W.11-12.10, CA.L.11-12.1b

WRITING PROMPT

Think about the heroes in the selections you have read. What qualities define a hero, and how does a legendary hero help shape the history of a nation? Write a narrative about a hero (or heroine) modeled on the style of *Le Morte d'Arthur* or *Beowulf*. You can write about a real, heroic person you know, or you can write about a fictional character. You can set your narrative in a real or imagined world.

Your narrative should include:

- an engaging opening that introduces the characters and setting
- vivid descriptions of the setting and characters
- a logically organized sequence of events
- an ending that effectively wraps up the story
- an underlying theme or message

You've already made progress toward writing your own hero narrative. You've thought about your purpose and audience, and organized ideas. You've explored narrative techniques you can use and have sequenced events in the plot. You've roughed out ideas for your introduction and conclusion. Now it's time to write a draft of your narrative.

Use your Story Structure Map and your other prewriting materials to help you as you write. Remember that narrative writing begins with an introduction that introduces the characters, setting, and conflict. Body paragraphs develop the plot with events and descriptive details. Transitions help the reader follow the sequence of events. A concluding paragraph resolves the conflict and wraps up the story. An effective conclusion should leave a lasting impression on your readers.

When drafting, ask yourself these questions:

- How can I improve my introduction to make it more appealing?
- What can I do to make my hero come alive?
- How can I build the action or sequence the events and elements— including introducing and developing setting, character, or events— to make the story more interesting?
- Would dialogue or a different point of view make the characters or story more vivid?
- How well have I communicated my overall message, or theme?
- What final thought do I want to leave with my readers?

Before you submit your draft, read it over carefully. You want to be sure that you've responded to all aspects of the prompt.

NOTES

DESCRIPTIVE
DETAILS

sync•skills
Writing

SKILL:
DESCRIPTIVE
DETAILS

DEFINE

Descriptive details make writing more specific and help readers visualize a narrative. They convey a vivid picture of the experiences, events, setting, and characters in a narrative using **sensory language,** which appeals to one or more of the five senses (sight, hearing, touch, taste, and smell).

IDENTIFICATION AND APPLICATION

- Descriptive details help readers visualize key story elements:
  › characters (what they look like and how they act)
  › **direct characterization:** The writer makes explicit statements about a character and what that character experiences.
  › **indirect characterization:** The writer reveals a character through his or her words, thoughts, and actions and through what other characters think and say about the character.
  › setting (the time, location, and culture the narrative is set in)
  › plot events (including plot development and conflict)
- Writers use strong adjectives to clarify descriptions and to help readers better understand and visualize the story.
- Sensory language engages readers and helps them better understand the experiences described in a narrative. It creates **imagery - the "word pictures"** that writers create to elicit an emotional response.

MODEL

In the excerpt from *Le Morte d'Arthur,* Thomas Malory creates a vivid scene:

> Upon Trinity Sunday at night **King Arthur dreamed a wonderful dream,** and that was this: it seemed that he saw **upon a platform a chair and the chair was fastened to a wheel;** thereupon King Arthur sat in **the**

richest cloth of gold that might be made. And the king thought that under him, far from him was **hideous deep black water;** therein were all manner of **serpents and worms and wild beasts, foul and horrible.** Suddenly **the king thought that the wheel turned upside-down and he fell among the serpents, and every beast caught him by a limb.** The king cried out as he lay in his bed and slept, "Help, help!"

The **event** is made clear at the start of this passage, "King Arthur dreamed a wonderful dream." Malory's use of the adjective "wonderful" suggests that this dream is important.

In this description of the dream, Malory says that King Arthur is seated "upon a platform a chair and the chair was fastened to a wheel." Below him is "hideous deep black water" and "serpents and worms and wild beasts, foul and horrible." This provides the reader with a strong image of the **setting.**

Arthur is described to be wearing "the richest cloth of gold that might be made," and this description serves to directly **characterize** him — showing that Arthur is very powerful and wealthy.

He **experiences** trauma in this dream, and Malory uses strong descriptive details and sensory language to convey it to the reader — "the king thought that the wheel turned upside-down and he fell among the serpents and every beast caught him by a limb." This description is rich with detail and sensory language — notably the sense of touch shown through the beasts grabbing Arthur's arms and legs. (Imagine how much less powerful this scene would be if Malory had just written, "Arthur had a nightmare about snakes"!)

 PRACTICE

Choose a paragraph or section from the draft of your narrative writing. Think about how you might incorporate descriptive details into the paragraph or scene that would appeal to one of the five senses. When you are finished, trade with a partner and offer each other feedback. What added dimension or meaning do these descriptive details provide? Do they enhance a character's traits or provide additional information that help you to visualize the setting? Can you distinguish examples of either direct or indirect characterization in the revised selection? Provide each other with helpful feedback and suggestions on how to improve and strengthen your revisions.

NOTES

REVISE

CA-CCSS: CA.W.11-12.4, CA.W.11-12.5, CA.W.11-12.6, CA.W.11-12.9a, CA.SL.11-12.1, CA.SL.11-12.2, CA.L.11-12.2a

WRITING PROMPT

Think about the heroes in the selections you have read. What qualities define a hero, and how does a legendary hero help shape the history of a nation? Write a narrative about a hero (or heroine) modeled on the style of *Le Morte d'Arthur* or *Beowulf*. You can write about a real, heroic person you know, or you can write about a fictional character. You can set your narrative in a real or imagined world.

Your narrative should include:

- an engaging opening that introduces the characters and setting
- vivid descriptions of the setting and characters
- a logically organized sequence of events
- an ending that effectively wraps up the story
- an underlying theme or message

You have written a draft of your hero narrative. You have also received input from your peers about how to improve it. Now you are going to revise your draft.

Here are some recommendations to help you revise.

- Review the suggestions made by your peers.
- Focus on the big picture first. Smaller details will be overlooked if readers are confused about the plot or the relationships between characters.
  › Revise your introduction if it isn't engaging or if it doesn't orient readers with the characters and setting and properly introduce the conflict.

> Check that the sequence of your narrative is clear and that the tone is appropriate. Add transition or time-order words to clarify any sections.
> Ensure that your conclusion reflects on the narrative and neatly wraps it up.
> Make sure your narrative has a theme or message.

- After you have revised elements of plot, think about descriptive details that will better help your readers visualize the story.
  > Do you need to add any descriptive details? For example, is there a detail about the setting that could help convey the mood?
  > Would adding dialogue help flesh out your characters? Dialogue can add life to your narrative.
  > Consider your narrator. Does the narrator have a clear voice? Is there anything additional he or she could share with the reader?

NOTES

EDIT, PROOFREAD, AND PUBLISH

CA-CCSS: CA.W.11-12.4, CA.W.11-12.5, CA.W.11-12.6, CA.W.11-12.9a, CA.SL.11-12.1, CA.SL.11-12.2, CA.L.11-12.2a

WRITING PROMPT

Think about the heroes in the selections you have read. What qualities define a hero, and how does a legendary hero help shape the history of a nation? Write a narrative about a hero (or heroine) modeled on the style of *Le Morte d'Arthur* or *Beowulf*. You can write about a real, heroic person you know, or you can write about a fictional character. You can set your narrative in a real or imagined world.

Your narrative should include:

- an engaging opening that introduces the characters and setting
- vivid descriptions of the setting and characters
- a logically organized sequence of events
- an ending that effectively wraps up the story
- an underlying theme or message

You have revised your hero narrative and received input from your peers on that revision. You have also explored ways to make your word choices more precise. Now it's time to edit and proofread your essay to produce a final version. Think about your writing process and all of the valuable suggestions from your peers. Ask yourself: Is my writing clear and coherent (does it make sense as you intend it)? Have I used descriptive details and precise language? What more can I do to improve my narrative's structure and organization?

- When you are satisfied with your work, move on to proofread it for grammar, punctuation, and spelling. Pay special attention to the parts of the essay that you just revised, because it is easy to introduce new errors or to accidentally create unclear sentences while proofreading and making last-minute corrections.
  - › Check that you have used correct punctuation for dialogue and have used all hyphens correctly. Be sure to correct any misspelled words.

> Be sure to apply your understanding of usage and its conventions to your writing of the narrative. Remember that you can resolve any issues by consulting references materials, as needed.
> Examine your understanding of syntax and your use of modifiers as you review your writing.
> Check the spelling of your work, remembering that while spell-checker is a valuable tool, it does not catch all spelling errors.

- Once you have made all your corrections, you are ready to submit and publish your work. You can distribute your writing to family and friends, hang it on a bulletin board, or post it on your blog. Be sure to include a list of the works you used for sources, and if you publish online, add links to those resources so that interested readers can gather more information. In addition, consider including art or images to illustrate your narrative.

Text Fulfillment
Through StudySync

If you are interested in specific titles, please fill out the form below and we will check availability through our partners.

ORDER DETAILS

Date:

TITLE	AUTHOR	Paperback/ Hardcover	Specific Edition *If Applicable*	Quantity

SHIPPING INFORMATION

Contact:

Title:

School/District:

Address Line 1:

Address Line 2:

Zip or Postal Code:

Phone:

Mobile:

Email:

BILLING INFORMATION   ☐ SAME AS SHIPPING

Contact:

Title:

School/District:

Address Line 1:

Address Line 2:

Zip or Postal Code:

Phone:

Mobile:

Email:

PAYMENT INFORMATION

CREDIT CARD

Name on Card:

Card Number: Expiration Date: Security Code:

PO

Purchase Order Number:

StudySync Text Fulfillment, BookheadEd Learning, LLC
610 Daniel Young Drive | Sonoma, CA 95476